Sophia Dunbar

A Family Tour Round the Coasts of Spain and Portugal

During the Winter of 1860-1861

Sophia Dunbar

A Family Tour Round the Coasts of Spain and Portugal
During the Winter of 1860-1861

ISBN/EAN: 9783337190835

Printed in Europe, USA, Canada, Australia, Japan

Cover: Foto ©Andreas Hilbeck / pixelio.de

More available books at **www.hansebooks.com**

A FAMILY TOUR

ROUND THE

COASTS OF SPAIN AND PORTUGAL

A FAMILY TOUR

ROUND THE

COASTS OF SPAIN AND PORTUGAL

DURING THE WINTER OF 1860-1861

BY

LADY DUNBAR

OF NORTHFIELD

WILLIAM BLACKWOOD AND SONS
EDINBURGH AND LONDON
MDCCCLXII

ADVERTISEMENT.

THE solicitations of some kind friends, and a wish to realise a few pounds for a charitable purpose, have induced the Authoress to publish the following Journal.

CONTENTS.

CHAPTER I.

PAGE

French hotels—Nismes and its antiquities—A Spanish diligence—First glimpses of Spain—Execrable roads—An overturn—A night at a railway station—Barcelona—Bad drainage—Deficient accommodation—The cathedral—Spanish currency—Spanish and English fashions—Spanish lace—A Spanish baptism—Adventure with banditti—Scenery round Barcelona—Manresa—A Spanish posada—Monserrat and the monastery—Ascent of the mountain—A Catalan landlord—Night accommodation—Martorel—Ancient bridge, . . . 1-26

CHAPTER II.

Routes to Valencia—A Spanish steamer—Arrival at Valencia—Churches and pictures—Church ceremonies—Cigar factory—The workwomen—Peasant costumes—Silk factory—The great hospital—Foundling hospital—Plaza de Toros—The fashion of Valencia—The scenery—Arrival at Alicante—Alicante—Love and jealousy—The date palm—The peasantry—The knife and its use—Soil and climate, ... 27-48

CHAPTER III.

Voyage to Malaga—Malaga—Hotels and accommodation—Light costumes—Scenery of the vicinity—Costumes of peasantry—The cathedral—Spanish sermons—Spanish justice—The brigand's fate—The fruits of Malaga—Turkeys and raisins—Outbreak of cholera—Start for Gibraltar—Spanish deceptions—Gibraltar—The convent garden—The dragon's blood palm—

CONTENTS. vii

St Michael's cave—Soldiers' home—Visit to Tangier—Tangier—A Tangier law case—The governor's castle—The governor's wife—The emperor's brother—The bazaar—A Jewish party—Farewell to Tangier—Return to Gibraltar, . . 49-79

CHAPTER IV.

From Malaga to Granada—The Vega of Granada—Hotels in Granada—The Alhambra—The Generalife—Restoration of the Alhambra—The gypsies' quarter—Sketching in Spain—The Cartuja convent—The cathedral—A review—A gypsy dance—Accommodation at Granada—A veteran—A Spanish home—Excursions from Granada—Mail cart travelling—Jaen and its population—The scenery—Night at Granada—A night arrival, ... 80-103

CHAPTER V.

A mule journey—Preparations for the road—Pinos—A village posada—Soto de Roma—Alcala la Real—Muleteers—Peasant costumes—An early start—Rearing of horses—Winter floods —Gibraltar to Cadiz—Murillo's St Catherine—Wine vaults of Xeres—The wines of Spain—Wines and their prices—Port wines, ... 104-121

CHAPTER VI.

Seville: Its houses and population—Public buildings—Murillo's paintings—Cigar manufactory—Foundling hospital—Story of a foundling—Life in Seville—Bull-fight costumes—A lodging-house—Washing establishment—Palm Sunday—The procession on Palm Sunday—Spanish revivals—Holy Thursday—The Infanta and her daughter—Ceremonies of the holy week—Washing the feet—The Miserere—Rending the veil—Easter Day, ... 122-145

CHAPTER VII.

The great fair—Life at the fair—The live stock—Bull-fights—The bulls—The fight—Character of the sport—A Portuguese bull-fight—Spanish sports—Spanish cruelty—Routes to Madrid—Cathedral of Cordova—The Guadalquivir—The Infanta and her husband, ... 146-162

CHAPTER VIII.

Arrival at Lisbon—Custom-house arrangements—Vestiges of the earthquake—Mosaics in the St Roque—Foundling hospital—Belem church—Portuguese churches—Modern aqueduct—Primitive vehicles—Railways and roads—Visit to Santarem—Chapel of Sta Rita—Portuguese navvies—Visit to Cintra—Moorish palace—Moorish remains—The Pena palace—Monserrat—Departure from Lisbon—Spanish bigotry—Curious shipment—Home, ... 163-184

TOUR OF A FAMILY

ROUND THE

COASTS OF SPAIN AND PORTUGAL.

———◆———

CHAPTER I.

Having determined to spend the winter in the south of Europe, after many interesting debates and conversations we decided that the south of Spain should be our destination. We had previously spent several winters at Nice and its neighbourhood, and we saw by the railway guides that it was now as easy to reach Barcelona by Perpignan as to go to Nice by Toulon.

We tried that all-powerful medium, an advertisement in the *Times*, for a servant who could speak the language, and were most fortunate in finding a Spanish female servant who had been sixteen years in an English family, and who proved of inestimable use and comfort to us.

We left Folkestone on the 27th of October, having allowed the first stormy break of the weather to pass, and then had a charming season for our journey, retreating south with the departing summer.

We had a smooth passage, and arrived in Paris the same evening without fatigue, and two days after made the journey to Lyons. It is better in France, when once upon the rail, to make a long journey and rest alternate days, than to attempt to break the journey by travelling short distances, because so much time is lost and fatigue experienced in all the tedious arrangements that are gone into at the stations for the weighing and the safety of the luggage.

It is prudent in France to inquire the price of one's rooms, as otherwise the people are apt to think that you are totally regardless of expense, and to charge accordingly. At the Grand Hotel de Lyon we were made to pay exceedingly high for our rooms. There are certain rooms on the first floor that are very expensive. After one day of rest, an easy day brought us on to Nismes : at Orange, half way to the latter place, stands a superb Roman arch, said to be two thousand years old. It can be seen from the railway, if people are on the alert, before reaching the station, but it is well worthy of a visit ; also it is necessary to be on the watch at the next station, as the ancient Palace of the Popes at Avignon is most imposing, as seen from the rail a few hundred yards before reaching the station. The ruins at Nismes are very extensive and interesting, including a grand amphitheatre, an idea of the size of which may be formed when it is known that the first Napoleon expelled two thousand inhabitants from under its arches in order to place it in its present state of cleanliness. It is so convenient as an arena that Spanish bull-fights have occasionally been held in it of late years ; indeed the " Plaza de Toros," at Valentia, which is a superb new edifice, although only in brick, is a close imitation of it. A temple here called the " Maison Carrée" is one of the most perfect and beautiful Roman buildings extant. There are interesting remains of baths, &c. There are excellent hotels at Nismes, Avignon, and Montpellier; the latter place is one hour by rail from Nismes; from thence to Perpignan is a short day's journey. The people are a diminutive race at Nismes, and onwards towards Spain; indeed, although an active, industrious people, they are not handsome. Vestiges of fever are seen in the lantern jaws and short-cut hair of many of the inhabitants of the whole of this south coast of France. There is a large extent of country under vineyards here, and many of the wines produced are full-bodied and good.

At Perpignan the traveller who is to journey into Spain is again obliged to betake himself to the old-fashioned mode of travelling by diligence, the railway north of Barcelona being opened only to Hostalrich and Mataro. We started in high spirits at the thought of our charming drive into Spain. We had a *mayoral* or guard, a driver, and two footmen. It was the duty of the latter to run alongside, to thrash the horses or mules, or to pelt them with stones when the road was bad, and to jump up and cling to the diligence when the road was so good as to enable them to strike into a trot. The approved plan of cross-

FIRST GLIMPSES OF SPAIN. 5

ing a river is to send the footmen in advance to move any large stones, or fill any holes either in the bed of the river or on the opposite bank; after which they return to the diligence, and the team is made to charge it at full gallop, accompanied with yelling, hooting, pelting, jolting, and splashing; and after a most exciting rush, if fortunate, you arrive safe, although breathless, at the opposite side. The men soon after begin to smoke and sing as if nothing had happened. The drive to Junquiera is pretty, passing El Boul and over the wooded heights of the Col de Pertûs and Bellegarde, the summit of the Pyrenean chain; you then descend to Junquiera, where is the Spanish custom-house; from thence the country is varied with cork-trees, stone-pines, and long-stretching plains where rice and *esparto* are cultivated; the latter is much used for making matting and ropes. To the west the Canigu, a fine mountain, spreads forth its spurs, the lower zone of which is covered with stone-pines; from this the distance is short to Figueras, where we slept and had our first specimen of a Catalan posada and its noisy inmates. The accommodation was scant and bad. The strong fortress of

Figueras is said to belong to the Spaniards in time of peace, and to the French in time of war.

We were on the following morning transferred by our traitor diligence agent to a smaller and dirtier diligence, and were told we must go on by this or return to Perpignan for redress. We got moodily into our small confined vehicle, and drove several hours through a cultivated plain to Gerona, which has a fine cathedral, leading up to which is a magnificent flight of eighty-six steps raised in 1607 by Bishop Zuazo. On leaving Gerona, our mayoral coolly told us we could not possibly reach the station in time for the train for Barcelona that night. The roads now became execrable, full of holes, heavy clay and mud, through which our mules struggled and plunged. Our diligence lurched like a ship at sea, and it became darker and darker. We felt very anxious as to our long lone road leading through rivers, mire, and mud; at one time we came to a dead stop, caused by eight mules being all down at once. After much confusion and noise, they were got up, and constrained by thrashing and abuse to renew the struggle; for some miles we continued to go on in the same manner, making some tremendous lurches, from which we miraculously recovered our balance; at last fortune deserted us, we lurched, quivered in the air for a second or two, and went over.

The diligence fell partly on a sloping bank, and we were not in a completely horizontal position, those who were uppermost were enabled to avoid crushing their neighbours to death. By the help of the mayoral we were dragged out one by one, and put down in the mud without any serious injury. There we were in the dark, but most thankful to be without broken bones. Our Spanish maid and the mayoral had been sitting in the front: they had made a flying somerset over the mules, and had lighted on the opposite bank; the former so confused with her fall, she could not at first answer to her name, and we were apprehensive that she had been killed on the spot, and were greatly relieved at last to hear, from beyond the mules, a feeble voice telling us she was not much injured. It was a curious fact that when the mules were all thus down in a confused heap, they lay motionless and harmless. A friendly lantern made its appearance in the hands of a man who had seen our downfall, and we all

8   A NIGHT AT A RAILWAY STATION.

trudged through the mire, and after half a mile's walk arrived at a temporary wooden station at Palma, two miles from Hostalrich, at 11 o'clock P.M. Here we were told there was no train till six o'clock the following morning, and no other shelter than this in the neighbourhood. The station was full of wild-looking Spaniards, congregated around small tables, drinking Catalan wine and coffee, and singing and making merry over it. They at first stared at us as interlopers, but soon got tired of that and continued their merriment. In the mean time we ingratiated ourselves with our hostess, who magnanimously offered to transfer a bedful of children to a darker and dirtier den, and put all the ladies of our party into their bed: this did not suit our ideas of comfort; we preferred waiting till the Spaniards retired, and then arranged to pass the night upon the tables and chairs, and rough it as well as we could, somewhat comforted by knowing that a strong guard of men had been placed around the station to protect ourselves as well as our luggage. We groaned on till morning, when we were enchanted with the unromantic sound of the railway whistle. We shook ourselves up, and with great satisfaction took our seats in a comfortable railway carriage for Barcelona, where we arrived in three hours.

Barcelona is a stirring manufacturing town, the Manchester of Spain; it has a fine harbour to the east, and is situated on a rich plain surrounded by swelling hills, and watered and irrigated by the river Llobregat, which falls into the sea to the south of Monjuich, a fine hill-fort which commands the town, and from which there is an extensive view. Through the centre of the town, leading from the port landwards, is the Rambla—a wide walk with seats and trees on either side, and at both sides a carriage thoroughfare. Here are the principal hotels, theatres, post-office, diligence-office, bureau for passports, best shops, &c. The Rambla is about three-quarters of a mile long; from it radiate narrow tortuous streets, with Prout-like houses jutting over the pavement in artistic taste, occasionally opening upon small plazas with fountains, at which groups of peasants are seen watering their mules, or carrying off their elegant-shaped earthen vases of water on their heads; and peeps of fine old Gothic churches, forming good subjects for an artist. The principal hotels are the *Cuatro Naciones* and the

Fonda de Oriente, both large ; the charge at the former was about 40 reals a-day, or 8s. 6d. English, for apartments and board for each person. The food was indifferent, and the house so offensive from want of modern improvements with regard to water and drainage, as to be totally unfit for persons accustomed to modern civilisation. The town lies so low that the drains cannot be properly flushed. The mode of making the main-drains in the centre of the narrow streets covered with pavement, in which there are large slits a foot and a half long by an inch wide, to allow rain-water to escape, also allows foul air to rise into the overhanging dwellings of the people. The Rambla is no exception in this respect, but being wider, the air is less contaminated. It is the only walk, and is certainly not air for delicate persons to inhale. The *Muralla del Mar* is a beautiful terrace-walk by the sea, but it is open to the same objection on account of the exhalation from the accumulated filth of the tideless port. The climate, certainly, we found delightful. In November the thermometer varied from 53° to 64° in the open air, while there was no sensation of cold in the house; and though there were fireplaces in several rooms of the hotel, we did not require to use them. Yet in spite of the climate, circumstances induced us to shorten our stay at Barcelona, where there are other drawbacks besides those mentioned above. It is almost impossible to hire a furnished house for the winter, it being derogatory to the dignity of a Spaniard to let his house; and there are no placards up to indicate that apartments will be let for immediate occupation, as in other parts of Europe. There is no English church, nor is the service even read in the Consul's house; indeed, there are numerous English workmen in the large manufactories, who have been totally neglected; the children born here, if baptised at all, fall into the hands of the Roman Catholic priests, and are lost to our Church, and their morals deteriorated by the temptations of a large and not over-religious community. Unfortunate seafaring men, both residents and those who visit the port in our ships, are without opportunity of attending divine service. Our countrymen in this respect seem shamefully neglected, which strengthens the opinion of Spaniards, that we, being beyond the pale of their Church, are totally without religion. We were frequently asked, in a hesitating whisper, if we were Christians. Were suburban villas built on the swelling hills outside the town, and a good hotel or hotels near the railway station, an English church erected, or the service read in the Consul's house, it is likely the English would flock to Barcelona, and find it a delightful winter residence. The town is sheltered, and there are numerous and interesting excursions to be made in the neighbourhood by railways and steamers.

The Cathedral *La Seu* is a grand Gothic building of 1298; a fine flight of steps leads up to it; it has two polygonal towers; the interior is lofty and solemn. The pillars which support the nave are of great solidity. The painted glass is richly-coloured and magnificent; the organs are large and fine toned; under each of them hangs an immense Saracen's head, with a long beard and gold earrings. These are frequently displayed in Spanish churches; they have had their origin in the wars between the Moors and the Christians. The cloisters adjoining are very beautiful; in the centre there is a garden in which are some date-palms. There are several other fine churches: La Santa Maria with a lofty single nave, the coloured glass in the windows of which church is very rich and jewel-like, was began in 1328 and finished in 1483. There is a good view of the exterior from the street facing the west end of it, with a fountain in the foreground. The oldest church in Barcelona is San Pere de los Puellos, built in 980. San Jacine, built in 1399, has a noble nave. *La Casa de Dusai* in the Calle de Regomer is a Moorish house, and has a fine courtyard ; and the *Cardonas* has a large and handsome patio or court. The Bishop's palace and that of the Counts of Barcelona are interesting. In the saloon of the *Audiencia* are the archives of Aragon, the finest in Spain, 8000 volumes, coming down to 874 ; they are said to be marvels of historical information, and are as yet almost unknown.

In travelling in Spain it is very necessary that some of the party should understand the language. In a country where everything is bargained for, those who do not understand it or the people, would be atrociously imposed upon. The use of Spanish money is at first confusing. It is advantageous to bear in mind that one hundred reals are equal to a guinea of our money, and a gold piece of that value is the current coin of the country. A sovereign is ninety-five reals; a crown, twenty-two reals; a shilling, four and three-fourth reals. It is best for ladies to wear black silk, or dresses of some dark colour. Bonnets are being introduced by the French; but hats are totally unknown to Spanish eyes, and cause the greatest consternation and astonishment. It was amusing to watch the countenances of mute amazement of those who met a lady wearing a hat; they would turn round, stand still, and gaze till she vanished from their sight. The streets of Barcelona being extremely dirty, we looped up our dresses; this caused the old women to rush out of their houses or shops at us, and pull vigorously at our skirts; it was difficult to appease them, or make them understand that our dresses were purposely worn so. The woollen mantas of Catalonia are very handsome. The men wear these over their shoulders much as Highlanders do a plaid. They are striped, the colours rich and brilliant, scarlet predominating. The price of these varies from four to eight dollars each. The *Plateria*, where they sell the gold and silver ornaments worn by the peasants, is worth visiting; the forms are elegant and quite antique.

The wines of the country are generally good. One cannot look for the best specimens at a hotel; but judging from those we had they are good, and that called *Priorata* seems a first-rate wine, and well adapted to the English market. We shall speak more fully of wines hereafter. There is a certain bird in this country, called *Estornino*, about the size of a quail, which feeds greedily on the olives; it is very fat and juicy, with a slight bitter taste; it seemed to us the most delicious of the feathered tribe. To turn one's taste another way, the beautiful lace of Barcelona must not be forgotten. It is made in the various villages around, generally in pieces, and sewed together at the lace establishments in Barcelona. It is cheaper here than elsewhere in Spain, and there is a great choice of pattern and quality. The white Spanish lace, similar to white blonde, is also made, but it is very expensive, and soon loses its colour, and can only be worn in very full dress.

We were never tired of visiting the beautiful cathedral, its cloister, and garden. We were fortunate enough one day after vespers, at 3 o'clock P.M., to see a baptism. A large merry party in full dress entered the cathedral, without any appearance of reverence or solemnity: the beaux of the party dipped their fingers in the holy water, and sprinkled it over the young ladies, they dodging to avoid it, and laughing indecorously. The godfather carried the *niña* (infant), which was only three days old: the godmother had a tall flaring candle in her hand. The priest met them at the door, asked the name of the child, said a prayer, took a stole from his neck and placed it on the infant's breast, then all walked to the font in a chapel at the left side of the door. At this moment one of the party asked us to join them, which we did. The infant's fine cap and frock being removed, the poor little red thing was seen swaddled up so tight it could not move, and its arms were extended like those of a distorted German doll. It was motionless, and had the appearance of being drugged. The priest took this atom of humanity in his arms, crossed its forehead, face, and breast, poured water over its head with its face downwards, turned it round, breathed upon its face, put salt into its nose and mouth, anointed its forehead, chin, and the nape of its neck with oil, took the huge candle from the god-mother, put it into the extended and distorted hand of the infant, placed a veil or hood on the child's head, all the time muttering a prayer with amazing rapidity. He put the lid on the font, took a book, inkstand, and pen from one of the attendants, and wrote the name of the child in it. This finished the ceremony. The godfather is expected to distribute money to a crowd of beggars, who always are on the look-out for these ceremonies, and assemble at the door; if they don't consider the donation sufficiently handsome, they call out "Stingy fellows!"

They are still a wild race around Barcelona, and many of these are seen in the town. A Spanish marquis was pointed out to us at the theatre, whose father, a banker, was said to have left him fourteen thousand a-year—a large fortune in Spain. The marquis is a strange, reserved man, and never goes into society; his only pleasure is the theatre. All these circumstances seem to have been well known to the banditti of the country, who formed the daring design of kidnapping him on his return from the theatre at night, and thereby extorting a large sum as a ransom. With this view they fell upon him and gagged him in one of the retired streets; but he was a powerful man, and made a desperate resistance; the noise brought the man-cook of a neighbouring house to his assistance. They two fought so resolutely that, although the marquis was severely wounded, he rescued himself from his assailants. A very large reward was offered for the apprehension of the miscreants, but they have never been discovered. The marquis continues to go to the theatre, but always accompanied by a strong guard.

We made a charming excursion to Manresa and Monserrat. We took the rail (which is open to Lerida on the Saragoza line) as far as Manresa station, which is two hours from Barcelona. We passed through a richly-cultivated plain. To the left, the jagged peaks of the singularly beautiful Monserrat rise clear out of an undulating country, covered with pines and brushwood. The river Llobregat winds round its base and through the valleys alongside the railway, which is well engineered, over and through rock that rises like a wall at each side, after which it opens out into a wider valley, at the right side of which rises the picturesque and beautifully-situated town of Manresa, crowned by its enormous cathedral. Its irregular houses, built on terraces of rock, are enlivened by wreaths of scarlet, green, and blue woollen cloth, hung on balconies across windows and streets. It is a thriving cloth-manufacturing town of more than 14,000 inhabitants. At this season the bright yellow of the Indian corn is superadded, the heads of which are strung on cord, and hung over balconies and around windows. This gives it a most brilliant effect. The station is more than a mile from the town, but as yet travelling by railway is in its infancy, and there are no conveyances to meet travellers; so we were obliged to hire a cart to carry our luggage up to the town, and we ascended on foot over a rough and ill-paved road to the Posada del Sol, where we were received with surprise, but with great civility. This was a good specimen of a common Spanish Posada. We entered it by a sort of vaulted stable or coach-house, where were muleteers unloading their mules. Through the archway beyond was seen a long vaulted stable, with about fifty mules, some kicking and braying. We ascended a narrow stair to the first floor, and found muleteers dining off olla, boiled beans, and white sauce, and drinking dark-red wine out of antique-looking glass bottles, with long narrow spouts, which they elevate high in the air, and a thin stream flows into their mouths, the lower lip being protruded to catch it—a fashion which it required considerable practice to excel in, and which we saw here for the first time. We had yet to ascend to the second floor, where we found some bare, primitive-looking rooms. Our landlady was very polite; and, pleased with the insinuating tongue of her countrywoman, our Spanish maid, she promised to cook us some of her best Spanish dishes for dinner : the result was a delicious dish of red-legged partridges, stewed with capsicums, and a savoury dish of kid and olives. The mosquitos were most annoying; travellers should come prepared with portable mosquito nets, for which Barcelona is famous. The accommodation was scant, and our sleep was driven away by these trumpeting tormentors, so we were not sorry to rise with the sun, and wander through this most interesting town. The interior of the cathedral is very grand, and the situation most commanding. The rushing streams through the town, and romantic situations of the houses and bridges, were very picturesque. The salt mines of Cardona, which lie some distance on the line of railway towards Saragoza, are said to be well worthy of a visit.

The following day we returned to the station of Monistrol, half-way back to Barcelona, where we got a *tartana*, a light two-wheeled covered cart, without springs, which was drawn by a stout mule, to take us to the village of Monistrol, three miles distant, which lies at the foot of the mountain of Monserrat. The hotel is a poor place; close to it is a fine Roman bridge. A French engineer told us it had been built on a very scientific principle. The bridge and town form a beautiful landscape for the artist. Upon the side of Monserrat, at the height of 3000 feet, stands the far-famed and much-revered monastery which takes its name from the mountain. The number of pilgrims during the summer is so great as to have induced the railway proprietors to construct a carriage-road to the convent from the station, a distance of eight or ten miles, at the cost of £20,000. From two to three hundred pilgrims visit it daily. In fine weather, a staff of nine diligences attends at the station of Monistrol, to meet the train which leaves Barcelona at a quarter to six o'clock in the morning, and arrives there at 9 A.M. They take passengers up to the convent, and return to meet the 5 P.M. train, which takes them back to Barcelona by 8 P.M. The season being past, we had to engage a private carriage, at the cost of 56 reals, to take us to the monastery. The road is smooth, admirably constructed, and resembles many of the alpine passes; the ascent is gradual, but long-continued; a parapet rarely occurs; single stones at a distance of five or six yards apart are the only safeguard; the precipices are almost perpendicular, and of an appalling depth. The air was cold and chilly, and singularly clear and rarefied. There is a fine extensive view of a country not pretty or interesting in itself, but rendered so by grandeur of space. The Pyrenees are seen in the distance, crowned with snow. The huge boulder-stones lying by the roadside looked like giants' work. The grand peaks above us took every form fancy can imagine—some like elephants or Nineveh bulls; others like giants on pinnacles in the form of sugar-loaves, seemed ready to topple over us. The lower part of the mountain is covered with arbutus, myrtle, heath, and boxwood. This mountain is celebrated for its flora. The convent is in ruins, the work of the French. One part only of the Benedictine con-

A CATALAN LANDLORD.

vent is inhabited by thirty-five monks, who keep a school for children of the higher ranks. The church has been partly restored, and painted in imitation of the Alhambra. The chief attraction is the image of a black Madonna. Her dress and wardrobe are very splendid, and can be seen on application.

We did not ascertain whether or not the Bishop of Barcelona is a shareholder in the railway, but we saw he offered large indulgences to those who come and say a certain number of prayers at some of the chapels here. The view from the terrace garden is very fine; also from a scrambling walk to the hermitage of Santa Ana and San Benito, near which is a singular fissure called La Roca estrecha.

We returned to our posada at Monistrol. Our landlord was a rough, coarse, short-nosed Catalan, cook and waiter all in one. He brought in our dinner of several well-cooked dishes one by one. After carving a dish he quietly sat down by us— viewed with satisfaction our good appetites—pressed us to partake freely—asked all sorts of questions as to our country, family, our impressions of Spain, &c. When one dish was finished he rushed away for another, and repeated the process. The chambermaid was a very rude specimen of her genus, who stared when we asked for any small luxury, such as water. Our rooms were devoid of comfort. In one there were five beds, one small basin, and two chairs; in another, three beds, one chair, and one table. Our nights were spent in execrating an atrocious watchman, who came his rounds every hour and thumped at the doors and windows to assure us of our safety, which caused a colony of dogs, who slept about the corridors, to rush down a flight of steps and bark and howl at him. Our safety might be established by this arrangement, but sleep was driven away. As soon as dawn approached, the muleteers, who slept below us, began their noisy preparations for the day's journey, so that we had a sorry night of it. While the monastic institution on the mountain above is on the wane, the handmaids of civilisation—manufactories—are springing up at the foot of it. There are several cotton-mills at the river-side; and we met a young man who had been enlightened by spending some months in Manchester to improve his knowledge of his profession.

Another excursion from Barcelona is to Martorel, one hour by rail to the south of Monserrat. The station is at the top of the Rambla. The country here for miles is a continued market-garden, with here and there a cotton manufactory in the suburbs of small villages. The first rising-ground at each side is of ugly red clay covered with vines and olives, while on the highest hills are ruined towers. Martorel is a straggling town —the principal street a sink of filth and mud two feet deep, through which mules heavily laden struggle; foot-passengers have to pick their way as best they can, close to the house doors. In some parts of Spain there are enactments to prevent the streets being cleaned on account of the value of the manure. The doorways are large and open, in which women sit making black lace, on cushions, on their knees. These unfortunate people inhale the effluvium from this pestilential mud which is constantly stirred up by the mules splashing through it. The people are ugly, coarse, and ill-made. The men's costume is unbecoming —trousers, which reach almost to their shoulders, and short brown woollen jackets—their heads covered with a purple or red woven night-cap, the long end hanging down behind, or doubled up over the forehead in a raffish sort of fashion. The women wear a tight-fitting square-made boddice of black velvet or cloth, and a bright-coloured cotton handkerchief tied round their head.

At a mile distant from the village there is a grand bridge, said to have been built by Hannibal. It has three arches, the centre one singularly lofty and pointed, 133 feet in span. On the top of this pointed arch is a peculiar gateway, rising from either parapet, apparently built to give sufficient weight to the top of the bridge, so as to resist the pressure upon the sides of the high arch. The width of the bridge is only five feet—barely sufficient for laden mules to cross it. At the east end of this bridge stands a Roman arch. This bridge widely differs from that at Monistrol, where there is a second blind arch built in at each side, to prevent the same side-pressure.

CHAPTER II.

There are three modes of going to Valencia from Barcelona. The land journey by diligence is long and fatiguing by Tarragona, Tortosa, and Murviedro (the ancient Saguntum). At all these towns there are fine Roman remains, and the cathedrals and churches are well worth visiting. The last-mentioned town (Murviedro) is only about twenty-four miles from Valencia, and can be visited from it either by diligence or in a tartana. There is a steamer from Barcelona once a-week to Valencia in about twenty hours; but if travellers wish to visit the Balearic Islands, it may be managed by taking a steamer, which sails in twelve hours to Port Mahon in Minorca; a second steamer touches at a small town in Majorca, opposite Minorca; a diligence will then take passengers from thence across the island to Palma, where steamers constantly call to take passengers to Valencia. We were told it is a very charming excursion. The islands are rich in orange gardens, fruit, and flowers. The people are civil to the English, whom they much resemble in their habits, and they are remarkably clean in their houses. Many of them speak English, and it is still taught in their schools.

On the 23d of November we embarked in the Tharsis, a Spanish steamer, for Valencia. We were summoned to be on board at 8 A.M., but we did not sail till 2 P.M. No sort of apology was offered, or even thought of, by any one concerned. The coast is pretty, the shores covered with sparkling white villages, and we had fine weather and a lovely moonlight night. We passed Tarragona late in the evening, and at six the following morning the Balearic Islands were distinctly visible, rising in detached rocks of deep purple against the rich glow of a rising sun; but when it came above the horizon the lovely phantom-like islands vanished. The coast becomes higher and more barren as one nears Murviedro and the modern town of Castillon de la Plana. We saw the ruins of the amphitheatre and town glittering in the sun. From this the hills gradually slope

ARRIVAL AT VALENCIA.

upwards, and, behind Valencia, form a semicircle, and rise again to Cape San Antonio to the south. The bay of Valencia is wide and open, and from it there is an extensive view of the town, with its domed churches and campaniles, which give it an Eastern appearance. We were obliged to land in small boats. On nearing the quay a swarm of wild amphibious-looking creatures closed round us, hanging on to the boat, crawling in over its sides, and when alongside seizing our luggage, screaming, and cuffing each other, and tumbling over packages in the most savage manner, like water-demons. With the assistance of a fellow-passenger, who had been long in Spain, we extricated ourselves and our luggage, and made our way through them. A second fight for ourselves and our luggage took place amongst the drivers of rickety carts and tartanas. At last we got ourselves and our effects to the custom-house, where there was not much trouble or delay, and again with difficulty succeeded in getting into a tartana. More money had been expended on its colours than on its springs; but our driver kept his balance on a little round seat, fastened to the shaft, in a most astonishing manner. It is fully two miles from *El Gras* (the port) to the town, the road wide but execrable. We went to the Hotel Madrid, where our rooms were tolerable, and food good. The bread throughout Spain is excellent. In the smallest village you may always procure good bread and chocolate; coffee is also generally to be had. The Fonda del Cid is said to be a good hotel; it is near the cathedral. Valencia is rich in churches and church ceremonies. None of the exteriors are imposing, but the interiors and pictures are very rich and beautiful. It is impossible here to give a list of the numerous works of Ribalta, Juanes, Ribera, and others; only some of those most striking to a stranger will be mentioned. In the cathedral, to the right on entering, in a side chapel, is a glorious "Christ," in a violet-coloured robe, and holding the chalice in his hand, by Juanes. In another chapel there is a fine Sapoferrato. In the Sacristia there are several of Juanes, Ribalta, and one Murillo ("The Entombment and the Maries"), also a "Holy Family," by Juanes.

From the bell tower is obtained the best view of Valencia, with its Eastern domes, tortuous streets, Moorish walls, and fine gateways; also of the

Huerta, a plain north of the town, which is perhaps the richest in Europe, extending to about sixty miles in length, and from ten to twenty miles in breadth. From the mildness of the climate, and from irrigation, it is under a succession of crops all the year round. This apparent earthly paradise, where oranges, olives, lemons, almonds, grapes, pomegranates, dates, Indian corn, rice, &c., abound, is treacherous, for hundreds of its inhabitants are swept off annually by fever. We counted thirty churches within the walls of the city. Near the cathedral is the chapel of Our Lady of the Unprotected, *Nuestra Senora de los Desemparados;* the image of the Virgin is literally a blaze of jewels, —a crown of pearls and diamonds, necklaces, brooches, and rings of every coloured jewel. One enormous emerald in a brooch which fastens the sleeve was given lately by the Queen of Spain. The infant Saviour in her arms is covered with similar jewels. The whole are worth £20,000; and the miraculous cures are wondrous. In the church of "San Juan," near the market, are two exquisite lamps suspended on each side of the altar from figures of boys on panthers. In this church is the celebrated "Concepcion" or "Purissima," by Juanes. In San Martin, on the left on entering, there is a fine picture of the Virgin, and a "Christ lamented by the Maries" underneath it. In the chapel of the Communion, out of the sacristia, there is a magnificent Virgin and Child with saints adoring, and angels' heads above.

The Chapel of the *Colegio de Corpus*, or del Patriarca, is celebrated for its ceremonies; at the Miserere, on Fridays at 10 A.M., is one of their most sacred ceremonies. We saw the dedication of flowers to the host in a silver tabernacle at this church. For this the interior is darkened, the altar only being brilliantly lighted up with fourteen enormous candles. Twelve priests in gorgeous robes, carrying pyramids of flowers in golden vases about a foot and a half high, enter from the sacristia. They stood in pairs before the altar, bowed themselves and their pyramids of flowers three times—first standing, then kneeling, then again standing. They ascended the flight of steps close to the altar, and there repeated the same ceremony, and placed their vases and flowers on the altar, and afterwards retired, six at each side. Meanwhile four priests, in rich crimson and gold-embroidered robes, and carrying the host, came

CIGAR FACTORY.

down the centre of the church, stood before the altar, and waved incense till the church was filled with it. The chanting and music during the whole ceremony were soft and beautiful.

In the Glorieta, a public garden, is the cigar manufactory: the building is handsome. We entered a Patio (or court), where they were unpacking cases of tobacco-leaves. They open one end of the cask, and turn out its contents, which look like a huge Brobdignag cheese. These are carried into a side vault, and weighed out; men in very scrimp apparel were chopping and mashing the leaves of tobacco to prepare it for smoking. On the first floor four thousand women and children were at work at long tables, making cigars. These are made by hand; the smaller leaves neatly rolled up and wrapped firmly round in a large tough leaf; it is twisted tightly at each end and gummed up; they are then tied together in dozens, and they retain their shape when dry. In the second room were tables, around each of which sat twenty women or children, all busy packing short tobacco for pipes. At the head of each table sat a woman, who weighed out the tobacco

C

and passed it down the table as quick as lightning to those who were ready for it. They pack the tobacco neatly into paper bags, containing each about a quarter of a pound. In another room they were making fine snuff, the stalks and veins of the leaves being carefully removed before they are rubbed down. It was curious to remark, in a large manufactory of this sort, the almost total absence of beauty amongst the young women. They had neither beauty of face nor of figure, and were of small stature. During our visit a bell was rung, and all those women who had infants went down to the principal entrance, where the children were brought to them; they sat down on benches or on the ground, and nursed their half-famished-looking babes, after which they returned to their work. A good workwoman cannot make more than two and a half reals a-day, or about sevenpence of our money. The whole is a government monopoly, from which there is a large profit.

The market is large, and teems with delicious fruit and vegetables. The peasants' costume is most becoming: the men wear very full white linen drawers, black or bright-coloured velvet jackets, richly braided; the gayest of waistcoats, red fajas (sashes), white cotton stockings, and hempen sandals; on their heads, the pretty round turban-like black velvet hats; across one shoulder, a striped woollen manta of the brightest colours. The women dress their hair in a most becoming manner: a rich roll of plaited hair round their heads, pierced with silver pins with large knobs. The mules and donkeys are decked out with worsted tassels and trappings of every hue, and, when carrying panniers of golden fruit, form, with the peasants, the most beautiful groups for an artist. The mantas here are very beautiful; they vary in price from one hundred to four hundred reals—in other words, from one to four guineas.

Señor Monsenat, one of the professors of the College, to whom we had an introduction, was exceedingly kind, and offered to show us everything of interest. We first visited with him the silk manufactory. There were one hundred and fifty women employed in preparing the cocoons for winding off the silk. They have long troughs filled with scalding water, into which they throw the cocoons, which float for some minutes; they then turn them over and round till they are thoroughly scalded; in this process they are constantly burning the points of their fingers, and, as a ready antidote, each person has a basin of cold water, into which they constantly dip their fingers; thus the pain and any permanent ill effects are immediately removed. When the cocoons are thoroughly scalded, they pass them to others, who wind off the silk in skeins. That first wound off is coarse, and is only used for sewing-silk; the second is more abundant and finer, and is sent into an upper chamber to be wound upon reels. Five cocoons make one skein of silk. The machinery in this manufactory is French, and the director of the establishment is a Frenchman.

We next visited the Hospital, the largest in Spain. The Valencians say it is the admiration of all Europe. It is built in the form of a cross; four very long wards radiate from the centre: at this point stands an enormous stove, the heat of which is diffused by pipes to the farther end of each of the wards. This renders the air wholesome and dry; but little artificial heat is required in this climate. The iron bedsteads and bedding are scrupulously clean; the blankets, checked scarlet and white, give it a gay cheerful look. Above the head of each bed is an open cupboard filled with shelves for books, work, or refreshing drink for the patient during the night. Between every two beds is hung a tent-curtain on a circular rod, to enable the patients to dress in private: none could see this without perceiving its great advantage and comfort in point of decency. The kitchen is airy, large, and clean; in the centre is a huge copper for boiling water; at one side there are three coppers for preparing *olio*, a soupe-maigre for the idiots, who are under the same roof, but kept apart, and are carefully attended to by Sisters of Charity. There is a separate room for bread, in which were standing long lines of baskets full of fresh bread of the best quality. They have a machine for cutting bread into slices for soup; four loaves are put into it at one time. The rooms for female convalescents are neatly matted, and have chintz curtains to the beds; at the end of the room there is a small chapel and altar. The men's convalescent ward is quite as clean, but not so much furnished. We saw a priest with the Host going to administer the last sacrament to a dying inmate.

We next visited *La Cuna*, or the Foundling Hospital, containing five hundred unfortunate children. On entering the Patio we heard a distant sound, as of innumerable litters of puppies whining; on nearer approach it turned into a deafening and piteous wail of helpless infants; they all seemed to want to be nursed at the same time—and it is very possible they did so, seeing that only one wet nurse is allowed for three or four infants. The long ward was divided down the centre by two rows of stone pillars; at each side of these, in a double row, were placed cradles on stands, each containing an infant. The bedding was clean, and a muslin curtain thrown over the crib to protect the infant from mosquitoes. It was piteous to hear the continued wail. We raised the muslin curtains of several of the cribs. The pinched-up features of the sleeping, and restless tossing of the crying, were most painful to see and hear. These infants were from three to ten days old; they are then sent to the country to be reared. At eight or ten years of age, if not reclaimed or adopted into the family where they were nursed, they are sent to charity-schools to remain till they get employment. We could not learn whether the mortality was great, or whether or not they turned out well when they arrived at years of discretion. We omitted to say that near the entrance-gate there is a turning-box, into which the unnatural parents place their infants : a matron attends in a room immediately behind this ready to receive them.

There is in Valencia a modern Plaza de Toros, or amphitheatre, for bull-fights. It is of enormous size, built of brick, and looks as if it would contain twenty thousand spectators. An English merchant who had resided four years in Spain told us the Spaniards are cruel to each other, and to their beasts of burden : he attributes much of it to the scenes of blood at their bull-fights.

The *Audiencia* has a finely-carved roof and some frescoes of 1599 ; also a fine wooden gallery around it. In a second room, the *Secretaria de Gobierno,* there is a richly-gilded ceiling, the ground of which is a pale blue, the gilding and colour as fresh as if newly painted.

At the Glorieta, or public garden, in the Alameda, all the beauty and fashion of Valencia appear daily towards sunset. The Alameda is a beautiful shaded avenue, with a promenade on each side; here the world drive slowly up and down to see and be seen in their high-wheeled gaily-painted tartanas. Four-wheeled carriages are only just beginning to appear in Valencia, and there are few streets in which they can drive. The very large wheels of the tartanas enable them alone to go along the streets full of deep holes, large stones, and other impediments. We found it less fatiguing to walk than to submit to be shaken in these conveyances, although they are clean, the drivers civil, and the fares moderate. In this respect Valencia is very far behind Seville. During our stay there the temperature was generally about 64° in the open air, and 60° in our rooms.

We left Valencia for Alicante on the 30th of November. We started at 5 A.M. by rail for Alicante; the moon shone brightly; the watchmen were lighting their small fires on the pavement and heating coffee. At the railway station a man with a large coffee-urn and a basket full

THE SCENERY.

of cups and saucers and rolls of bread (lantern in hand), offered travellers a cup of hot coffee for rather more than a farthing English, and a roll of bread for a halfpenny. This struck us as an excellent arrangement where there is no refreshment room, and is a preventive against drinking ardent spirits. It was very cold till the sun rose. We could scarcely see the rich huerta till we arrived at the first station; there the fine carob-trees and olives appeared to be of a magnificent size—almonds, vines, melons, Indian corn, extensive rice-grounds and mulberry groves; in fact, all and everything for the well-supplied market of Valencia. The curious *norias* (water-wheels) in this district are most picturesque.

At Alcira, the next station, there were large orange-trees thirty feet high, full of golden fruit, and extensive groves of date-palms. At Tativa the rivers Albarda and Guadainar dispense much fertility around. The town is finely situated on the side of a hill looking to the north; the hill is crowned by a Moorish castle. It is a favourite resort for the Valencians during the summer months, but it is well worthy of a visit at any season, as the climate is delicious. From this to Almanza the country is bleak—a long chain of bare grey hills with troops of goats attended by goatherds dressed in rough brown serge. These hills are singularly upheaved and full of caves. At Almanza, half-way to Madrid from Valencia, is a Moorish castle on a conical hill; the town nestles at its base. In the distance there is a hill resembling Salisbury Crags near Edinburgh.

We breakfasted at the station, and met the train coming from Madrid for Alicante; the one we had come by proceeded to Madrid, which place it reaches in fourteen hours from Valencia. The line of rail south now took us through a most interesting country. The romantic towns of Villeña, Sax, and Monavoe, with their fine old castles backed by high mountains, form the most charming views for an artist.

On approaching Alicante the country becomes arid and Eastern-looking. Soon the high rock of Alicante appeared in sight, and we arrived there at 2 P.M. The Fonda el Vapor of better repute being full, we went to the Fonda Barcelona, where the accommodation was dirty and the food bad. Alicante is a beautifully situated town, but the streets are so tortuous and crooked that we saw no house in which a respectable party could find an abode, excepting the house of the English Consul. We had letters of introduction from one consul to another over the south of Spain, from all of whom we met with the greatest kindness and attention. There is a large hotel being built close to the harbour, which will be a great improvement on any accommodation that the town can afford at present; but being on a level with the sea, and overlooking a tideless harbour, a lengthened residence here would not be advisable. On account of the railway being open to Madrid from Alicante, it has become of much more importance and wealth as a seaport.

The season was too far advanced at this time for us to venture to Madrid, as the cold is very intense there in the winter months. We were much amused with a semi-imbecile waiter at our hotel, the proportions of whose limbs and mind were singularly ill developed, his head being of an enormous size. He was in love with the chambermaid, or she had designs upon him, both circumstances so extraordinary, it might be either way. Another lover of this nymph of broomsticks looked in and invited her to accompany him to the café to be treated: while they were partaking of some refreshment, the first lover rushed in with a large open knife in his hand, and threatened to cut her throat if she did not instantly return with him to the hotel; also demanding the restitution of the presents he had given her in moments of weakness, especially of a certain red cotton dress: the neighbours interfered, and with some difficulty restored peace. Our Spanish maid was in great anxiety as to the future conduct of the parties. She was much relieved, a short time after, to see that the young lady, mop in hand, had got the better of her jealous lover, and was administering a severe beating to the imbecile.

From Alicante an easy day's excursion can be made to Elche and its palm forests. It is about eighteen miles distant. Here the date-palm is cultivated for its fruit. It is so profitable that they are extending the plantation very much, and already there are about ten square miles of it. It consists mostly of rows of date-palms surrounding squares of ground about a quarter of an acre each, in which corn, lucerne, and pomegranates are cultivated. Sometimes the palms form beau-

THE DATE PALM.

tiful avenues, with a broad footpath between the rows. Many of the trees were from forty to fifty feet high. We were fortunate in **seeing** them in great beauty, full of orange-coloured fruit almost ripe. The peasants were engaged gathering the **ripest.** They seem to run up the tall branchless trees with the greatest facility. They use a rope made of the esparto grass, upon which they can place the greatest reliance as to **strength.** They enclose themselves and the stem **of the tree in a large loop,** which enables them **to stand** about two feet apart from **the tree. They** then pass this loop across the small of their back, and lean against it with their whole weight, then jerk their body forward and raise the loop about eighteen inches upon the rough stem of **the** palm-tree, and lie well back; they again **raise** their feet eighteen inches up the stem, so **that they jerk and** step alternately, until they arrive at the top of the tree where the fruit grows. When there, **they** continue to lie back **on the** rope by which **they** ascended, and gather **the** fruit into a basket suspended by a cord from their shoulders. The **male** palm bears a large cluster **of white** flowers which **look** like carved ivory; these are enclosed in a rich dark-brown sheath till they burst forth in November, and form a most lovely circle round the head of the palm. The female palm bears large clusters of fruit from bright orange-coloured stems that break out from the head of the palms under the fan-like leaves. The barren trees yield a large profit in leaves, which, by tying up together, are bleached and become a pale straw-colour. They are then sold throughout Spain for the processions on Palm Sunday, and they are also hung up against houses to prevent the ill effects of lightning.

The peasants, with their bright striped shirts, white linen drawers, red sashes, and little black velvet hats, their sheds built of palm-leaves and Indian corn, antique-looking earthen jars, the norias where mules and donkeys are engaged drawing water, all form the most perfect groups for a picture. A quantity of dates is now exported to England and elsewhere as African dates. We were invited to enter a peasant's house; it was beautifully clean, and even tastefully ornamented. They were very civil; asked us to accept of their house, themselves, their all; of course, not meaning us to accept of it. One of the party so gained the affection of the mother of the family that she presented her with a piece of gold leaf the angels had showered down upon the Virgin in a procession the last great fête-day.

The road from Alicante to Elche was most atrocious. We dashed through holes, over long sliding rocks, through dried beds of rivers; and sometimes the road was so destroyed by the late rains that we were obliged to drive in the neighbouring field, and in again to the road with a tremendous jerk that sent our heads to the roof of the carriage. The dust was most stifling, and we looked like millers' men. One of our coachmen dropped accidentally a strong silver-mounted cuchillo. We found they each had one. That belonging to the second was a woman's dagger. Upon inquiry we found it belonged to the gallant coachman's lady-love, who had proved rather a dangerous character, and he had thought it prudent to get possession of it till she was in a milder mood. The evening previous to our arrival at Alicante a man had been stabbed to death in the street. He himself had on a previous occasion committed the same crime. We had two coachmen, one to drive the wheelers, the other the leaders, besides a boy to run alongside to thrash and throw stones at the mules or horses. The climate of Alicante seems excellent. The country around it is barren. Where rock does not project through, the soil is generally strong grey clay, which in winter, when the cereal crops are removed, has a bleak and ugly appearance.

CHAPTER III.

On the 2d of December we embarked for Malaga at 11 A.M. The weather was like a fine summer's day in England. We sailed in a Spanish boat not particularly clean. The Spanish passengers spat like savages even in the cabin. The captain was greatly enraged at having been sent away from Alicante with cheap bad coal, which proved the principal cause of a tedious passage. That evening we passed close by Cartagena and Almeria. Both places, we were told, are most interesting to visit. The following morning we passed Adra, Motril, and Velez Malaga. The first range of hills along this coast is covered with terraces of vineyards. The snowy chain of the Sierra-Nevada ought to have been visible, but a thick mist obscured our view of it. Near Velez Malaga there is a fine bridge or aqueduct, and a cascade falling direct into the sea. There are several cotton manufac-

D

tories here, with their tall chimneys. We entered the harbour of Malaga at about seven o'clock in the evening, after a thirty-two hours' passage. In landing so late we missed the advantage of seeing the town from the sea, which is said to be the most imposing view of it.

We shall now proceed to describe Malaga. The streets are generally narrow and much crowded; many of the Moorish houses yet remain; it is, however, clean and well kept, and the people on the whole are well housed. The Alameda is a broad avenue for pedestrians, with two rows of trees and seats, and a carriage-road on each side. This runs from the port to the river, a distance of about three-quarters of a mile. Here are situated all the wealthy merchants' houses and the hotels. The ground on which the whole of this part of the town is built, has been reclaimed from, or thrown up by, the sea, within the last two centuries. The Moorish walls do not enclose this part of the town, which is at no great elevation above the level of the sea. It has been originally ill-drained, and perhaps from the nature of the ground would still be difficult to drain well. From this cause, and the circumstances of there being no tide in the port at one end, and the river being sometimes flooded and sometimes dry at the other, the sanitary effect of the otherwise charming climate of Malaga is greatly counteracted. The hotels generally are bad, and few in number. The *Alameda*, which is the best house, from defective drainage or some such cause, was the seat of a large proportion of the cases of cholera and fever that occurred during the winter. There was a very good suite of rooms at the Oriente Hotel, the landlord of which was most obliging and civil. At the Victoria Hotel, next door to it, there are also some suites of rooms to the south. We only heard of one good house that was let to strangers during the winter : no other could be met with; in fact, there is very little accommodation here for delicate or respectable people. It is much to be regretted that in such a heavenly climate, and with the advantages which will be seen in the sequel, no commodious hotels and villas should be built: in a healthy suburb, for example on the road to Granada, there are spots on which the most charming hotels or villas could be built. In the crowded streets of the old town there seem to be no houses that would accommodate strangers. The climate is very mild during the winter; the thermometer ranged from 62° to 70° in our south rooms without fire.

We may mention an incident illustrating the mildness of this part of Spain. In a village about two miles out of the town, we were amused with the scanty garments of the children, which consisted of a cotton shirt reaching to a little below the waist; we were still more amused at hearing that these were their winter garments, and that in summer they wore nothing. A benevolent English lady who resided one summer in this village, surprised the children one Sunday morning by presenting each with a neat comfortable cotton suit, in which they figured with great delight all Sunday; on the following day, however, she saw them all turned out again in a state of nature. On calling upon some of the mothers, they told her that they were extremely obliged to her for her kindness, but they could be no party to such extravagance as allowing the children to continue to wear them, and they contemplated turning them to better account.

The Alameda is a fashionable promenade on

fête-days and festivals, and some handsome carriages appear on the drive around it; in fact, carriages are much confined to the town, as most of the roads are only passable a short distance out of it. Divine service is performed in the house of the English Vice-Consul: it is most admirably and efficiently conducted by a highly esteemed clergyman. Nothing can exceed the civility, kindness, and attention of the English consul to his countrymen who visit Malaga. Although the drives are circumscribed, the rides are varied and interesting, amongst vine-clad hills, peasants' farms, and the threshing-floors and yards for drying the far-famed Malaga raisins. These yards are placed on a slope facing the sun; they are about forty feet long and fifteen broad, surrounded by a wall a foot high. The inside of this is strewn with sand, and divided into compartments by narrow footpaths, between which the bunches of grapes are laid to dry, after being previously allowed to wither a little, by having the stalk half cut through on the parent stem before being gathered. They require from ten to fourteen days to dry; they are then packed in boxes and sent to the merchants in the town of Malaga.

The peasants ride from their homes on the neighbouring hills to transact business, and to attend the market, on smart little Andalusian horses. The men are good-looking, and gaily dressed in regular Spanish costume; and they are always armed with a rifle, which is hung by their side. Their costume is very becoming: a black velvet jacket, ornamented with bunches of silver buttons; a red sash, in which is placed the cuchillo or knife; tight-fitting knee-breeches of some bright colour; leather gaiters beautifully stitched in patterns, and laced up with leather tags; and a little round hat, the foundation of which is made of wood and covered with black felt, the brim turned up all round, and covered with black velvet; two round tufts of silk are placed at the side. The horses are as well got up as their riders. The saddles are large, and have a high pommel in front; over these is thrown a leather saddle-cloth embroidered with worsted, trimmed round with a deep fringe, and large tassels at the four corners—the head-gear much ornamented with fringes, tassels, and bells. We were told that the Andalusians spend much money upon their dress; a full costume for fête-days will often cost from £20 to £30. They will deny themselves even necessaries of life to obtain it. In the Calle de las Cainas there are excellent shops for mule and horse trappings, and also for mantas and gaiters.

The churches at Malaga are uninteresting. The Cathedral is an enormous building of unsightly architecture, which looks too large for the surrounding town; the interior is very capacious. On Christmas Eve we were present at the midnight mass; the Cathedral was brilliantly lighted up, and a band of music, mostly composed of violins, played several pieces of beautiful music, principally from operas. At 1 A.M., the mass being concluded, the organ pealed forth, and imitated successively an infant's cry, the cock's crow, the donkey's bray, and the ox's low. We saw a smile on many faces. It was profane, and painful to our feelings. In returning at 2 A.M. to our hotel we found the streets crowded, many parties singing The Shepherds' Hymn very sweetly, accompanied by guitars and tambourines. All was decorous, and we saw no appearance of drunkenness.

We went one day to hear a sermon addressed

in particular to young women. The priest gave them much good advice, and said, "Good conduct would adorn them much more than finery in dress; it would not only be more pleasing to the Almighty, but would also be much more admired by the young men." On another occasion we went to hear a sermon, where the priest began by inviting very particularly the attention of his audience, and said if they would listen attentively, he would give them twenty days' indulgence. The Roman Church in Spain is very despotic and intolerant; the civil law of the country even is much more lenient. The Church exercises great control, if not over the press, over those who write for the press, and the whole population are subjected to the confessional. We heard that young men complain that they are obliged to confess, otherwise means are taken to greatly prejudice mothers and daughters against them.

We visited the jail, containing about 330 inmates; the majority were men, but a large number both of men and women were incarcerated for cases of stabbing. People here all carry long Andalusian knives, and avenge themselves on slight provocation. Justice in Spain is easily avoided;

a Spaniard told us that the balance always fell to the side where there was gold. Besides which, he said, "If there was no assassination or stabbing, what would become of the priests and lawyers?" Many of their quarrels are from jealousy, and originate at their dances. We saw some fandango-dancing on the sea-shore. At Christmas the town population pic-nic by the seaside, and each little party has a basket of provisions, a guitar and castanets. They dance fandangos with a great deal of attitudinising and gesture. When a handsome woman dances, those who are captivated by her charms throw their hats at her feet. We first saw one or two young women who created no sensation; at last, rather a handsome girl stood up, and she had not danced many minutes surrounded by her friends and her rivals, when a shower of hats were pitched at her feet. Her triumph was almost too great for human nature. She was much overpowered by her blushes for some minutes; at last she recovered herself, and went on in triumph. The custom of throwing hats at the feet of a handsome woman is not confined to the dance; our Spanish maid, although no longer in her teens, was a handsome woman, and generally so complete in her costume that she attracted admiration, and on several occasions we saw a hat pitched at her feet accompanied by a pretty speech, with which she was not a little gratified. She was not fond of our being present at the fandango-dancing, as quarrels sometimes ensue, and she hurried our return home. Her fears were not groundless, for, about an hour after, a young man was carried into the town mortally wounded.

On one occasion we were shown a lone posada resorted to by muleteers, where a few years ago a desperate struggle and fight had taken place. It happened that two farmers came from the country to sell sheep at a fair; when they had realised their cash by the sale of their flocks, a desperate brigand acquaintance wished, whether they would or not, to have the money from them in loan, which they absolutely refused. On the evening of the same day he came to them at this little inn, shut himself up into the same room, and declared that if they did not hand over the money to him he would put them to death on the spot. He had mistaken his men: all carry knives in Spain; these were soon brought out on this occasion. The two men rushed upon him, fortunately proved victorious, and in self-defence put him to death. The police got wind of it, but the men refused to deliver themselves up or remove a barricade at the door until the Governor of Malaga should be present, to whom they said they were prepared to surrender. The Governor was sent for, and soon came to the posada; he heard their case, received their explanations on the spot, pronounced it justifiable homicide, and the men were allowed to return to their homes.

There is a Plaza de Toros or amphitheatre here for bull-fights, but it is a poor building, and there was no bull-fight during our stay. There is a very large café (La Suéza) for the million, where tea, coffee, or ice, with newspapers, music, and company, can be had for the small sum of $2\frac{1}{2}$d., or one réal Spanish. It is an institution much to be admired.

We arrived in Malaga too late for its far-famed grapes, or most varieties of its fruits. We had pomegranates, quinces, oranges, dates in abundance, and most kinds of provisions seemed sufficiently abundant. During the summer the inhabitants eat large quantities of the prickly pear, which grows here in every direction. At Christmas, large flocks of turkeys were driven in hundreds into the town by peasants, with long bamboo-canes in their hands. It was said that every family who could afford it had a turkey for dinner on Christmas Day. In the hotel we had abundance for a week before and a week after.

Malaga raisins are worthy of their renown; one merchant, to whom we had an introduction, said he had exported four hundred thousand boxes, each containing from twenty-three to twenty-five pounds weight of raisins; this is one-third of the whole annual exportation from this place. It is a curious instance of the want of integrity in Spain, that these boxes are all received from the growers as containing twenty-five pounds weight, but they are invariably about two pounds short of the full weight. Our friend told us he could only trade with the people by winking at this deception.

We witnessed an amusing scene here. On the anniversary of the day on which some revolutionists had been executed, about thirty years since, for demanding concessions from government that have since been granted, there was a procession to

OUTBREAK OF CHOLERA.

the graves of these poor men, whom they considered martyrs. This liberal party filled half-a-dozen carriages ; but in order to render the procession as imposing as possible, they were preceded by a mounted trumpeter in gold lace and scarlet, with a cocked-hat and gold-headed mace. This is evidently an old Spanish fashion which must have been known to our ancestors ; no doubt many of our beaux and belles must regret that it has become obsolete. Young men in long beards or short kilts, and young ladies in small hats or large crinolines, might double the sensation they create if they were allowed the advantage of a trumpeter in front.

During the month of June 1860 cholera had visited Malaga, and prevailed to some extent for six weeks, and then for a time disappeared, until Sunday the 10th of August, when a heavy cloud and fog hung over the town during the day and succeeding night : most wonderful to relate, it was found next morning that there had been about eight hundred cases of cholera during the night ; of these, forty-eight proved fatal the first day, and forty the second day ; a few cases were afterwards fatal ; and the malady was then said to have disappeared. The authorities are very sensitive on this point, and although Malaga is reputed to be the most unhealthy Spanish port in the Mediterranean, they continue, if possible, to have it understood that their port is free from infectious diseases. For example, when an English gentleman died there during our residence, being an M.P., the Consul wished to telegraph to the English government that he had died of cholera; but the Governor would not allow this to be done, and insisted on his only telegraphing that he had died suddenly. In the beginning of January, so many of our friends were taken ill of cholera and fever that we took alarm. Some of our party went to Gibraltar and some to Granada.

On the 8th of January, the party going to Gibraltar were told to lose no time, but to secure berths on board a good Spanish steam-boat that was to sail for Algeciras at five o'clock in the afternoon, and reach that place at five the following morning, in time to catch the morning boat from Algeciras to Gibraltar. We got ready in a hurry and went down to the pier at the appointed hour, but we found that we might return to the hotel again, as the steamer would not sail till nine at night. When we lamented the chance of missing the boat from Algeciras to Gibraltar next morning, we were assured it was of little consequence, as we should catch the afternoon boat, and land at Gibraltar at a very convenient hour. On our appearing again at the pier at nine o'clock, the boatmen all required to be paid double, because they had been twice in attendance. This is quite after the fashion of Spain. We sailed before morning, and had a smooth passage, and reached Algeciras at 2 P.M., where we were told on the best authority that we had been deceived, for that no afternoon steamer had sailed from that port for Gibraltar for many months. We lingered from 2 till 4 P.M. in vain endeavours to find a good sailing-boat. It was now considered too late to reach Gibraltar before gunfire; we were consequently obliged to sleep at Algeciras in a third-rate inn, and to cross by the steamer next morning before breakfast, having been detained thirty-six hours on a voyage that a good English steamer would have performed in eight.

The view of Gibraltar from the sea is very beautiful and picturesque. On landing, we were struck with the substantial fortifications, the beautiful state of the roads, the cleanliness of the town, and the large and burly forms of the artillerymen. We looked around us with great satisfaction. The Rock of Gibraltar is about two miles and a half long, by half a mile broad. There is a low shelf along the whole west side, from twenty to fifty feet high, on the northern end of which the town is built; the rest is occupied by barracks, parade-ground, gardens, and officers' quarters. The top of the rock is 1450 feet high. The whole place is in beautiful order, and bristling with artillery in every direction. The duties of the military are as strict as during war. After dark or gun-fire, the sentinels fire without ceremony on any boat that moves within reach. The surface of the rock is mostly covered with loose stones and decomposed rock, out of which springs an abundant variety of trees, shrubs, and flowers; the palmetto is very abundant. Eagles are sometimes seen, and the red-legged partridge, the linnet and goldfinch, abound. No shooting is allowed on the rock. There are also still some monkeys, but they are only to be seen early in the morning; during the day, they go to the high sheltered and sunny crevices of the rocks, but during the night they are fond of robbing orchards, like monkeys at home, and venture down amongst those around the town. It is believed that in consequence many have been poisoned, and hence the smallness of their number. There are also some foxes on the rock; a sergeant of one of the regiments told us that the sentries at Catlin Bay said they frequently saw them on a fine summer's morning taking a swim in the sea. The Alameda, a parade-ground just outside the town, is well wooded with stone-pines, carob or locust trees, and olives. It is one of the most beautiful terraces in Europe, and commands an enchanting view of Algeciras, the Strait of Gibraltar, and the African coast and mountains.

One of the sights of Gibraltar is the beautiful garden attached to the residence of the Governor, which is called the Convent. In it are one or two fine date-palm trees, which, however, do not mature their fruit in consequence of their vicinity to the sea. The banana, a lower-growing plant, owing to the protection afforded by the walls, ripens its fruit, which is to be seen hanging in clusters. There are some large orange-trees, which, in the winter time, are covered with white blossom, and fill the air with perfume. Against the house, there is a Brazilian creeper, called Bugainvillæa, which is one of the most gorgeous plants imaginable; it was a complete mass of rich colour, something between magenta and maroon. There are other rare plants in the garden, which is a most enjoyable spot; but the grand sight and admiration of botanists is the dragon's-blood palm; it is about thirty feet high, having a stem of twenty feet. It is supposed to be more than a thousand years old, and to have been planted by the monks on this spot, which was for many centuries their garden. In the month of February it was covered with large clusters of dark orange-coloured berries, which were not food for man, but could not have been poisonous, seeing that a large flock of sparrows were busily engaged in eating them daily.

There are various singular and extensive caverns in the rock, or more properly mountain, of Gibraltar. At the south, near the residence of the Chief Justice, there are some that have only been partly explored, and these seem to have communication with the sea. In one of these, lately discovered

ST MICHAEL'S CAVE.

from above, was found the skeleton of a human being, with the skull on the hand, indicating that some unfortunate mariner, in times long gone by, had here found a resting place more terrible than a watery grave. First amongst the caves that are well known is St Michael's, which, although standing nearly a thousand feet above the level of the sea, is rendered magnificent by its stalactite pillars and beautiful white incrustation, deposited on all sides of the rock by the dropping of water which leaves this deposit. The entrance to it is low and narrow, and consequently the cave cannot be well seen without considerable trouble and expense in artificial light. On hearing one day that the officers of the royal artillery intended to light up the cave for a party of friends, we signified our great desire to join, and we were kindly invited to be of the party. After a severe climb on a very hot day in February, we reached the mouth of the cave, where a large merry party of gentlemen and ladies, young and old, had assembled. Some steps had been cut in the earth and mud at the mouth of the cave, and these again had been covered with palmetto leaves, in order to keep the ladies' boots dry. The ladies descended each with the hand or the arm of a gentleman, down these sloping steps for about twenty feet to the bottom of the cave, which then stretched away horizontally. The interior is very grand, about forty or fifty feet high. On the right hand was a fine stalactite pillar resembling a date-palm, which reached to the roof; a second pillar looked like a gigantic monument. The cave was magnificently lighted up with coloured lights, which were scientifically managed by some men of the artillery, and the effect was very striking. Further to the right was a second cave, which resembled the chapter-house of a cathedral. The stalactites, suspended from the roof, appeared like the arches in the Alhambra. It is singular, at such a height above the level of the sea, that this cave should be completely drenched with filtering water. Very extensive caves of difficult access are said to branch away from this one. Some years ago, an Engineer officer, in spite of the water, mud, and intricate passages, endeavoured to explore them, and led a party of men who contrived to crawl upon their hands and knees a considerable distance: finally, the officer stuck so fast that he was with great difficulty extricated by his men, with the assistance of ropes.

An interesting sight at Gibraltar is a soldiers' home or club. This has been lately established by a philanthropic Artillery officer. It is a large and commodious house of several stories. There are coffee-rooms, reading and writing rooms, a lecture-room, billiard-room, with tables arranged in it for chess, draughts, and other such games. There were upwards of 3000 subscribers at one penny each a-week. Breakfast with tea or coffee, bread, butter, and eggs, costs threepence. The whole was most orderly, and highly appreciated by the men. The authorities are so satisfied with its success, that they have intimated their intention of repaying its founder several hundred pounds which he had expended in establishing it.

Good hotels and good houses are the only things wanting in Gibraltar: a large family find great difficulty in getting lodged. From Gibraltar many interesting excursions can be made. The ride to the cork wood has an endless charm. The garrison keep a subscription pack of fox-hounds. We believe the association with English sport is more charming than the reality, for the ground is very rough, and the sport is said to be indifferent as compared with English hunting. Another favourite excursion is to Ronda : it is romantically beautiful, has a grand annual fair, and is celebrated for its bull-fights.

San Roque, only seven miles from Gibraltar, is a prettily situated town on the way to the cork wood. There is a good carriage-road to it, and a comfortable house for a large family might be had at a moderate rent. The climate is delightful.

Perhaps the most interesting excursion of all is to Tangier, on the African coast. Our kind naval and military friends put it in our power to make the trip in a small government steamer. We sailed after breakfast, and in three hours arrived there. We spent the night in Africa, and returned the next afternoon. On reaching the African coast, we found there was no pier. Robust odorous Arabs stood up to their waists in the water ready to carry us through the surf hoisted upon chairs, each person being supported between two bearers ; in this way we reached the sandy beach. We passed through hundreds of idle people, and under a gateway into the main street of the town. Here was novelty indeed !— society in its most primitive and rude state, such as could hardly have existed in Europe for the last thousand years. It may be said there are no streets; there are zig-zag alleys between the houses, and perfect kennels of dirt; we saw two dead cats and other enormities in them. About one fourth of the population appeared to be black, perhaps another fourth half-caste, a fourth Jews, and the remaining fourth handsome large fine-looking Moors, scarcely darker than Europeans. The houses appear comfortable inside; the roofs are flat and commodious, with a parapet, and are the usual resort of all the inmates as the sun goes down. The beasts of burden here are mostly camels. Everything bespeaks a different quarter of the globe. The town of Tangier is built on two hills; the one nearest the sea is crowned by the alcazar (the castle) and the palace of the emperor's brother; narrow, steep, winding streets cross the hollow to the second hill, where are the bazaar, the mosques, the Jews' houses, and the market-place.

The mosques have square towers ornamented with green and white tiles; on the top is a narrow minaret surmounted by a flag-staff, upon which a colour is run up to announce to the world below the hour of prayer; at the same time a man from the roof near the minaret proclaims the hour, and calls them to prayer. Formerly all were obliged to discontinue their work and kneel down and pray; this is now no longer obligatory.

We ascended, and visited the Governor's castle. On our way, two wild-looking men rushed up past us, reviling each other, and on our arrival at the courtyard we found the Deputy-Governor sitting on his heels on the step of the stair at his door, hearing the case of these disputants. The two men knelt before him and spoke alternately; he looked stern and sensible. He was a middle-aged man of fine countenance. He heard all they had to say, and gave judgment in a brief sentence. When he had done so, the disputants jumped up, one walked away quietly, apparently the successful pleader, the other tossed his arms wildly in the air, and shouted as if he were a lost man.

In the courtyard were picketed about a dozen of the emperor's cavalry horses, poor miserable beasts; they appeared more suited for sand-carts than to carry a trooper. The military were not distinguished from the civilians, excepting by a high-peaked red cap like a strawberry pottle. They had greatly the advantage over the horses, for they appeared to be handsome, tall, powerful men. The governor was absent, but some of his wives and children were there. We entered the castle by a fine Moorish gateway, with the remains of Arabic tracery and inscriptions, still beautiful, but much disfigured by whitewash; the inlaid wood of the roof was much injured. In this gateway on stone seats sat two fine-looking Moors, *à la Turque*, writing orders. The patio is large, and paved with green, blue, black, and yellow tiles. We saw the governor's sleeping apartment, arranged luxuriously with rugs and carpets; purple and scarlet silk robes were hung from nails in the wall; a sword, bell, inkstand, and other nicknacks lay on a richly inlaid mother-of-pearl and tortoiseshell table, raised about a foot from the ground, and placed by the side of the couch and rugs. We went into the baker's department, entering out of the same patio; four jet black women were sitting on their heels round a very low circular table, kneading the dough in large flat china basins; it seemed strange not to see the dough turn black in passing through their fingers. They grinned and smiled most good-humouredly, and pointed to two other black women who were nursing two polished jet-black babies, and seemed to wish we should admire them. Several other youthful specimens were running in and out. They wore scanty red flannel dresses tied tightly round their necks, and with very short sleeves, which showed to advantage their round black arms. With some difficulty we persuaded the inmates to let us see one of the governor's wives. We were shown into a long narrow chamber, destitute of furniture, save a few rugs opposite the door, and a charcoal brazier, with a dish of vegetables simmering in an earthen jar upon it. Near the brazier stood a tall slight Moorish woman, who on seeing us fled, like a frightened hare, into a dark corner, covering the lower part of her face with the folds of muslin that were hanging round her like a veil. We could only see a pair of dark eyes gleaming at us, but they were promising of beauty. As we could not converse with her, we bowed and retired.

In the afternoon we were taken by a kind friend to the palace of the emperor's brother, and presented to him. He lived in a dilapidated palace near the alcazar; the entrance to it is through a narrow Moorish gateway, where some fine-looking Arab guards were placed. The patio was full of orange-trees and flowering shrubs. A black usher and a handsome Moor were in attendance. The usher went to announce our arrival; and soon after, we were told to ascend the stairs and enter the prince's suite of apartments. At one side of a patio and under an alcove sat Muley Abbas, brother and viceroy of the Emperor of Morocco, not on a rug or ottoman, as we expected, but in an arm-chair. He is a fine-looking man, about forty-five years of age; his complexion is dark, but not black. He wore a rich blue dress, much embroidered with gold, a white turban, and many yards of gauze-like white muslin folded round him, here and there showing the rich dress beneath. He was very polite to us, shook hands with us, and, through the medium of the friend who presented us, made a few civil speeches, after which we retired. It was a strange scene of mingled grandeur and dilapidation.

The bazaar is a street with open shops at either side. Each shop has a wide shelf all round it. On the side next to the street either one or two Moors sit *à la Turque*, with all their goods on the shelves around them; they hand these down to their customers without moving from their seats. There is a wooden shutter which is let down during the day, and forms a kind of table; at night it is raised and locked; the only entrance is through the open window, which is about three feet from the level of the street. The only articles we saw of native manufacture were finely engraved and painted brass trays, embroidered shoes and slippers, and some long Moorish guns; we bought some of the former, but the long gun-barrels were too clumsy to carry off.

When we were making our purchases in the bazaar, the crowd suddenly opened, and, to our horror, we saw a criminal who had committed murder undergoing his sentence, led by two soldiers. Immediately behind him was a third soldier, with a knotted rope in his hand. The man was stripped to his waist, his hands were tied across his breast, his back was purple and streaming with blood, his countenance was pale and full of agony; he was to be taken from jail weekly, and to receive four hundred lashes each

A JEWISH PARTY.

time until he died. This scene haunted us for days after.

We were fortunate in soon observing a more pleasing incident. The Jews are rich here, and have handsome houses and live in comfort. The Jewesses are very handsome, and are not darker than Englishwomen. They have fine dark eyes, and singularly pencilled eyebrows, with delicate features. We were taken to see a party which had assembled at one of these houses, to celebrate with music and feasting the performance of a domestic religious ceremony. The family, with numerous relations and friends, were congregated in a small room richly furnished; on the bed at one end of it reclined a handsome Jewess with her infant by her side. She wore a gold handkerchief folded round her head, and fastened on the forehead with a golden ornament; two long sprays of jewels hung down at each side of her face. She wore long earrings and a splendid necklace; her robe was black, with gold and crimson trimming. Another very lovely and gorgeously dressed Jewess sat on a rich carpet in the centre of the room, surrounded by friends both male and female. They had instruments of music, and appeared to be chanting a sort of hymn. Trays of sweetmeats were handed about amongst the guests.

We also visited another Jewess who lived in a very comfortable house, the patio of which was beautifully clean, and prettily paved with coloured tiles, and had a fountain playing in the centre. The lady of the house showed us into her receiving room, said she felt much honoured by our visit, and made us sit down and rest. She wore a black silk robe embroidered with crimson silk, and on her head a scarlet and gold handkerchief fastened in front with a large gold brooch.

We were very sorry not to be able to spend another day at Tangier, but we were obliged to return with our steamer before dark. The anchorage is not good in the Bay of Tangier, and we had to reach the steamer in a small boat that was knocked about by the surf. Each of the party was carried into the boat on a chair supported on each side by Moors; on reaching the stern of the boat, they suddenly raised the chair in front, which caused the feet to be carried over the edge, and as suddenly lowering it, the party was shot forward on their feet, or on all-fours, as the chance might be.

Running out from the point at the foot of the walls of Tangier, is a long ridge of half-sunken rocks, over which the angry waves were surging and boiling. We had to row close to these in order to avoid the swell, which gave a feeling of insecurity and danger, the more so as our bare-legged Moors kept up a chattering argument as to our best course, thereby neglecting their oars, and causing the boat to waver from side to side. It was a great relief at last, to find ourselves by the side of our trim little government steamer, and still greater, when on board, to see the quiet steady English sailors doing their work without comment or hurry. Notwithstanding a head wind, in three hours and a half we landed at Gibraltar.

CHAPTER IV.

Two of our party who went to Granada engaged the coupé of the diligence that left Malaga at 4 P.M. on the 10th of January, and reached Granada at noon next day, a drive of nineteen hours. The fare is twenty-five pesetas, or about £1 English, for each seat; but having to travel all night, it was found advantageous to take the third seat in the coupé, to give more room, and to prevent the possibility of being incommoded by a disagreeable fellow-passenger. Having to ascend to a great height soon after leaving Malaga, we had fourteen mules to our diligence. The road circled and wound up the mountain, over a red clay soil, where aloes, prickly pears, and vines were the sole produce of the otherwise bare hills. Looking back towards the south, the view was very grand; Malaga appeared immediately below us. At the summit, as the light failed us, we were met by an armed guard, who mounted the diligence, and proceeded with us for our protection during the night. After passing the first high chain of hills, we entered wild valleys of bare rocks, at whose base were chestnut groves, and soon after we began to descend to the beautifully situated town of Loja, with its ruined Moorish castle and church standing on an eminence. Here we were refreshed with a cup of chocolate and a roll of bread. At daylight we entered the rich Vega or plain of Granada, where we soon came in sight of the Sierra-Nevada towards the south, and on the other hand the Elvira hills. The floods of December had left marked traces; half of the town of Santa Fé had been utterly destroyed; houses had been carried away, and banks of mud left in their stead. The road had been cleared of the débris of the river Xenil which traverses this plain.

We were now in sight of the hill of the Alhambra and the town of Granada. This distant view of it is not imposing, but it becomes more striking as we approach. We entered the town of Granada with its Moorish towers, gateways, and narrow streets, and its wild-looking population, and passed on to the Alameda Hotel near the junction of the

F

rivers Darro and Xenil. Here there is a good view of the Alameda and the Sierra-Nevada beyond. The far famed Alhambra is a mile and a half from the town; and having heard that the hotels there were comfortable though primitive, we preferred their locality to those in the town, and immediately proceeded thither. We were fortunate in finding clean neat rooms in the Fonda de los Siete Suelos, at the foot of one of the Alhambra towers. The Fonda Ortiz, opposite, is equally good, and both are moderate in their charges. This was not the season in which travellers usually venture into this high district; but fearing we might not be able to visit it later, we had determined to brave the cold. The nights were chilly, the thermometer varying from 46° to 50° in the house; but during the day the sun was hot. There is one advantage at this season, namely, that the snowy range of the Sierra is seen in great beauty.

It is not easy to describe the Alhambra, or enter into particulars as to each individual part of its extensive courts, towers, gateways, &c. In Ford's *Spain*, a most excellent historical account is given of it; also in the romantic volumes of Washington Irving's *Conquest of Granada*, and his *Tales of the Alhambra*. The Alhambra is built on a spur of the Sierra-Nevada, as Ford describes it, in the form of a grand piano, the narrow end being turned towards the town of Granada, and overlooking it. The whole of this is enclosed by the red towers and walls of the Alhambra. In ascending from the town we passed through the gateway *de las Granadas*, built by Charles V.: passing through this, three paths diverge; that to the right leads to the red towers, the centre walk leads through the avenue of elms to the public gardens; the third turns to the left, and leads to the principal entrance of the Alhambra, the *Torre de Justicia*. It is a tall, red gateway; over the outer horse-shoe arch over the door is carved an open hand, the emblem of hospitality; over the inner arch a key is carved, the symbol of power. Passing through this gateway, we entered a narrow lane, leading past the *Torre del vino* to the *Plaza de los Algebes*, under which are the Moorish cisterns, still in daily use. This plaza separates the *Torre de la Vela* from the Alhambra and Charles V.'s most ill-placed, unfinished palace. From the Torre de la Vela the view of the Vega and the surrounding mountains at sunset is glorious. The entrance to the Alhambra, where the porter resides, is by the side of Charles V.'s palace. On entering the courts and corridors, the marble pillars and arches, the honeycomb ceilings, are a perfect bewilderment of beauty. The soft, creamy tint of the elegant tracery, and the brilliant touches of gilding, are most lovely. The Ambassador's Hall is magnificent; through its deeply-recessed open windows are seen the distant mountains, the river Darro, the hill covered with cactus and aloes, amongst which you see the caverns of the gypsies and the Moorish palace *el Generalife*, the palace to which the Moors who became Christians retired after their expulsion from the Alhambra. The court of Lions is like carved ivory, and is very beautiful; but its fountain, although of respectable Moorish origin, is most ungraceful. Its lumpy lions look sullen and out of character with the fairy-like corridors around them. The mosque and *Mihrab* (the sanctuary where the Koran was formerly hung) are very beautiful and richly ornamented. In a recess in the Sala de Justicia is a splendid china vase about five feet high; it has an Arabic

THE GENERALIFE.

inscription upon it, and some quaint figures, half birds, half beasts. One handle has unfortunately been broken off. It was found by the Spaniards, after the expulsion of the Moors, full of gold dust out of the Darro. The Infanta's Towers, and the small mosque in a garden near, are well worth a visit.

So much mischief has been done by unprincipled visitors breaking off the stucco tracery and carrying off porcelain tiles as reminiscences, that an order has been given by the governor not to allow any one to go through the Alhambra without a guide. We, however, gained the confidence of the principal guide, who allowed us, during our stay of a fortnight, to wander about it alone, which added greatly to the charm and enjoyment of its beauties.

The Generalife, the palace of Boabdil's son, is about half a mile distant. Its fine old cypress avenue leads up to the entrance of a fanciful garden. The water from the Darro here flows through numberless streams to irrigate the garden; it is then carried across a ravine by a fine aqueduct into the Alhambra, where it supplies innumerable streams, tanks, and fountains. There are some fine ceilings and arabesque tracery in the Generalife Palace; the view from it overlooking the Alhambra is very beautiful.

During the present winter, and for some years past, the Alhambra has been undergoing restoration under the charge of Señor Contreras, a Spaniard. It is admirably done; the new additions are scarcely to be distinguished from the old Moorish work. There is yet much to accomplish in order even to preserve what is left. Señor Contreras has made casts in plaster, which give the most perfect idea of the colour and delicate tracery of many of the most beautiful bits. Some large models of the interior of the Alhambra have been sent to Russia by Señor Contreras to be exhibited at St Petersburg at the expected exhibition of 1862. We also met Monsieur Bachan, a Russian artist, who, with a friend, was making paintings of the coloured tiles, stucco tracery, roofs, &c., for the same exhibition. M. Bachan is a first-rate artist; his views of the cathedrals and architectural subjects in Spain are beautifully and carefully executed; also his costumes of the peasantry are most accurate.

The neighbourhood of Granada is full of interest. We paid the gypsies' quarter a visit. The view from it of the Alhambra is fine. In sketching it, we were surrounded by specimens of rich-coloured gypsy women, with shining coal-black hair and polished mahogany-tinted skins. They wore apricot-coloured flannel skirts, trimmed with dark crimson cloth vandyked, black velvet boddices, green plaid shawls, and, round their heads, red handkerchiefs. They were fit studies for an artist. The men were tall and powerful, dark and dangerous-looking. They scowled at us from under their slouched hats. Their dress resembled the Spanish *majo* costume, rich brown predominating in the colour of the cloth of their apparel. The children, imps worthy of such parents, peered and peeped from every hole and corner concealed by cactus and aloes, and shrieked out ill words at us. The men and women begged incessantly, and soon became so troublesome and importunate that we were obliged to retreat with half-finished sketches.

It requires great temper and patience to sketch in any part of Spain. The people are so uncivilised, and so full of child-like curiosity, that they collect around one; even peasants passing on horseback stop, dismount, and lead their horses up to the circle gathered round any person sketching. They talk most volubly to each other, make observations as to your object and intentions, examine minutely your paper, pencils, and dress, ask innumerable questions, and being unaccustomed to truthful answers, generally conceive that you have been endeavouring to lead them astray, and consequently arrive at conclusions entirely at variance with the truth. On one occasion, a sturdy peasant, who showed no wish to be uncivil, was so entirely overcome by his curiosity, that, on seeing a rich shade of colour put upon a water-colour drawing, he uttered a long, loud, drawling exclamation, rubbed his large hand completely across it, and then held up his blue fingers for the edification of his neighbours. Another took the sketch-book forcibly from our hands, gazed at it, passed it round the circle, and then returned it with a polite " gracias."

In crossing the narrow streets leading from the gypsy quarter into the town of Granada, to go to the *Cartuja* convent, we were completely hemmed in by a wild-looking crowd, amongst whom were many gypsies. A savage youth, with a scowling bad countenance, brushed rudely past us to the side of an equally unpromising-looking subject, who had an open Andalusian knife in his hand, saying, "Why don't you cut their throats? they are English ladies!" The Spanish maid understood them, and immediately threatened them with "justice" (a word in Spain equivalent to punishment), if they dared to touch us. Finding out his mistake, he said, "I don't wish to cut a Spaniard's throat, only that of your companion, for she is English."

We hurried out of this bad neighbourhood. When we arrived at the Cartuja convent, two miles distant from Granada, we found a fresh batch of gypsies sitting in circles near the walls of the convent; one group on the steps before the door of the church were playing upon guitars, singing, and playing cards. These were mostly men, and they wore very short black velvet or cloth jackets, with a bright coloured cloth sewed in patterns upon it, and embroidered round the edge of the pattern with gold-thread. The church of the Cartuja is full of relics. The sacristia is rich in jasper, and in inlaid tortoiseshell, ivory, and ebony wardrobes for the priests' vestments.

The doors of the sacristia are particularly handsome; they are very large and massive, and inlaid in the same rich manner as the wardrobes. The walk from this convent to the Monte Sacro, or Sacred Mount, commands a fine view of the Alhambra, the river Darro, and the extensive plain beyond Granada. There are many Moorish remains in the fine city of Granada, many of the churches very interesting, with tall bell-towers.

The cathedral was built on the site of an ancient mosque. It was begun in 1529. The dome is large; the general architecture is bad. In the interior the Coro, as in all Spanish churches, blocks up the heart of the central nave. There are seven fine pictures round the dome, painted by Alonzo Cano, who was a native of this town. The great sight of the cathedral is the royal chapel, containing the splendid alabaster monuments of Ferdinand and Isabella, side by side, and the equally beautiful monuments of their daughter Juana, and her husband Philip of Burgundy. The carving on all of these is most elaborate, the figures in deep repose, and the features exquisitely chiselled. We saw the purple velvet and gold robe embroidered by Queen Isabella, the casket which she gave Colum-

A REVIEW.

bus, full of gold, on his return from America, and a fine illuminated missal. We also saw Queen Isabella's crown, sceptre, and cross; also Philip's sword.

On the morning of the 23d of January, the birthday of the Prince of the Asturias, we saw a review on an alameda near the town of Granada. The general and his staff were well got up; the troopers small in stature, but good-looking young men. All the officers and men who had medals stood together, and the general passed by them, and particularly saluted them. We were struck by the silence of the crowd assembled to see them, —no vivas, no enthusiasm, they did not even speak to each other, a marvellous piece of self-denial for Spaniards, who are very loquacious; the only sound was that of the water-carriers, "Aqua buena," which was in great request, for although mid-winter the sun was very hot, so much so that one of the troopers fainted.

On another occasion we witnessed a *Funcion de Gitanos*, or gypsy-dance, got up by a large English party who came here. There were about twenty gipsy women and ten men. The females were dressed in bright-coloured cotton dresses, with deep flounces and crinolines, parti-coloured handkerchiefs over their shoulders, their greasy uncombed hair dressed with natural flowers. The captain of the party was a tall dark man, dressed like a Spanish peasant; he was a celebrated guitar player. The second in command was a tall slight man, of thirty years of age, in a majo dress, which is a black velvet jacket, very short at the back, to show off the faja or scarf worn round the waist, the jacket much trimmed with braid, black silk tassels, and bunches of silver buttons, sewed over it in every direction. The shirt is very full in front, and much embroidered; olive-coloured knee-breeches (a very tight fit) made of woven elastic silk, the sides of these trimmed with silver buttons, and finished off at the knee with a huge bow of scarlet ribbon; the legs below the knee encased in fawn-coloured leather gaiters, beautifully stitched in patterns, left open at the calf, and fastened above and below with leather tags; square-toed shoes, with brass nails; a little black turban-like velvet hat, with a turned-up brim, and tufts of black silk set jauntily on one side of his head, and which completed his attire. He was a celebrated tambourine player, and leant gracefully

A GYPSY DANCE.

against an open window, with his tambourine in his hand, ready to exhibit his powers when called upon. The captain opened the funcion or ceremony by playing some marches, and singing some songs well; after which two gypsy women got up and danced a fandango to the captain's guitar and the majo's tambourine; some of the gypsy men then joined in the dance; after this commenced the gypsy's dance. The captain and the majo, with their respective instruments, headed a column of women, who began to dance to a slow air played by the captain and majo. They followed each other in a circle round the room; presently they fell into the figure of eight, increasing their speed constantly to the tune of the music, till at last they got into a complete rush, and finished with a loud shout. The captain rested a short time, and played some beautiful marches on the guitar, sounding the harmonics clearly and distinctly; suddenly he jumped up, threw aside his guitar, seized the majo's tambourine, and played upon it by striking it against his knees, feet, elbows, head, shoulders, with various other antics, till he made the room vibrate. He looked like a man suddenly possessed by an evil spirit, except that his countenance remained calm and composed the whole time; he concluded with a sweeping bow and salute to the company, and sat down.

Granada is a charming residence for the spring and summer months. There is a good unfurnished house and garden to be let in the Alhambra, beside the little mosque. Many of the rooms in it have inlaid floors and ceilings, and arabesque tracery on the walls. It has a terrace overlooking the river Darro; a good garden, full of pomegranates, vines, and fruit trees; and all this is to be had for £3 a-month. There are also some rooms in the *Torre de Justicia* (the Tower of Justice) to be let, also unfurnished; but we were told furniture can be hired at a moderate rate from upholsterers in Granada. There is a large and commodious furnished house near the red towers, overlooking the plain of Granada and the Alhambra hills. This house has often been let to English families for the summer months.

The English vice-consul at Granada is most obliging and attentive to strangers, and would willingly read the English Church service in his house, if required to do so. There is a good doctor, of French extraction, Monsieur de Lagarde, professor at the College of Granada. He was educated in Italy.

We made acquaintance with the porter, his wife, and child, who lived in the Tower of Justice, at the entrance to the Alhambra. The former got this situation as a reward for his services in the expedition of the Spanish army against **Morocco**. He was one of the thirty-three who first entered Tetuan, and one of the three only of these who left it alive. He had a small pension of 2 reals a-day (or $5\frac{1}{2}$d. English). He eked out his livelihood by making hempen sandals, such as are usually worn by the Spanish peasantry, and called "alpargates." In our moonlight walks to the Alhambra in the calm quiet evenings, we used to pass through the Gate of Justice, which, like all Moorish gateways, is very high and **wide, and** of the peculiar form of **an S.** The wide end of the S, next to the Alhambra, is fitted up as a **chapel, with an altar, which** no four-footed animal in former times was allowed to pass. The opposite end, towards the exterior of the gateway, was fitted up as a porter's lodge, by having **a** space boarded off for our humble friend's sleeping apartment. A small corner, close to the paved foot road, was fitted up as a little workshop and kitchen. Here they lighted a wood fire on the pavement, and prepared their *olla* of vegetables for supper. An antique-looking lamp was hung from a rude iron hook fastened in the wall. The soldier sat at his low wooden table, and made sandals; his good little wife took out her work, generally some small article of dress for her child, that she had hushed to sleep, and placed in its bed behind the partition. We were so struck with the quiet happiness of these contented people, we often stopped and talked to them, and warmed ourselves at their bright blazing fire. They were much pleased with our visits, and asked us to sit down; and the soldier volunteered and told us all his adventures in Morocco, how he fought his way into Tetuan, and how he thought of his wife, and brought her back some small loot, that she might remember what a brave man her husband was.

There are many rides and drives into the mountain valleys around Granada. One to Lanjaron, by Sapio Reale, seven leagues distant, to which a carriage may be taken, is well worth making.

It is a Swiss-like village, famous for the beauty of its women, who are said to be of Moorish origin. It is also famous for the size of its olive, chestnut, and walnut trees. There is a small posada open for travellers during the summer months. Another ride is to Monachiel. When there, a local guide is necessary, to enable you to return by the mountain road of the Sierra-Nevada, which is said to be a very grand ride. There are also two bridle-roads to Malaga, one by Adra, the other by Velez Malaga; both are beautiful, and not difficult to accomplish in three days in fine weather. A guide and good mules can be got at Granada for these expeditions at a very moderate cost.

Two of our party, who travelled from Cordova to Bailen by diligence, found the only mode of proceeding that day or the following one to Granada, was to take the coréo or mail cart, a two-wheeled tartana with a pole, made curricle fashion, for two wheelers and one leader. It had no springs, but the seats were slung in the interior, like some of the Swiss waggons. At two o'clock in the afternoon the coréo called at the hotel for the lady and her maid, who were determined to get on at all risks, and who were obliged to submit to the ways of the country. There was no step to enable passengers to enter unassisted into the vehicle, but the postboy (we suppose in his usual fashion) went down on one knee just in front of the wheel, and told the lady to take a seat on his shoulder, that he might help her into her seat. She had no sooner done so than he rose to his full height with such a jerk as to throw her completely over all obstacles into the centre of the carriage. When this was accomplished, without a smile or further remark, he stooped down again, and requested the maid to follow the lady's example. She in her turn had no sooner done this than she came in, all arms and legs, upon the top of her mistress. Two minutes after, a respectable commercial traveller requested them to make room for him, as he was to be their fellow-passenger. He motioned them to take the best seats in the corners of the swinging seat, and then politely wedged himself down so firmly between them that they could with difficulty breathe. In another moment the gaudy conductor and the postboy were upon the front seat, and with a yell and a scream they were off at full gallop. For some little time we were in a breathless state of anxiety, from the rapidity of the pace, the apparent chance of an upset, and the excessive jolting. This went on for some hours, till we settled into a state of calm indifference as to our fate. Notwithstanding the rapid pace at which we travelled, our leader had no reins. Being accustomed to the road, and to gallop from one end of the stage to the other, he seemed quite at home, and showed the greatest sagacity in choosing the road, particularly when making the turns, when he would sometimes gallop to the very edge of the precipice, at others he would rush up close to the rock or bank at the opposite side, in order that he might keep a straight pull, and leave room for the wheelers and tartana to follow round the corner. The postboy screamed to his mules in a harsh voice, calling each by its name, such as captain, governor, good Christian, priest, poor curate, &c., and keeping up a most animated conversation with them, exhorting them to obedience and order. When they slackened their speed or turned restive, a perfect torrent of abusive epithets was hurled at them, such as "bad dog," "bad water," "Pontius Pilate," "thief," "vile Moor," "run, run, or I will put your mother under the earth," and many other curious imprecations. Indeed, we were told that it was fortunate for us that we had not a more comprehensive knowledge of the "manly" Spanish language.

At about six o'clock the fine old town of Jaen appeared in sight. It is situated at the foot of some high mountains, facing the north. At one side, on the first chain of hills, are the extensive ruins of a Moorish castle, whose yellow walls and fortifications extend down to the town, in the centre of which is an enormous cathedral, similar in architecture to that at Malaga, and having the same defect of appearing to overwhelm the town. The country around is very rich and fertile, and is much irrigated by old Moorish aqueducts and Norias. We stopped a quarter of an hour to deliver the mail-bags, during which time we strolled to the Alameda or public walk. The inhabitants appeared a race of large handsome cutthroat-looking people; there were many gypsies amongst them. The women's costume is most becoming, consisting of a dark-blue cotton dress, made very short in the skirt, and edged with narrow frills; a crimson cloth mantilla, edged

THE SCENERY. 101

with black velvet, thrown gracefully across their shoulders and partly covering the back of the head.

In a short time we were again summoned to mount our post-boy's shoulder, and to take our places in the tartana, and started as before at full gallop. The country for many miles was exceedingly pretty,—very extensive orchards in the valleys through which we passed. The higher hills were covered with cork and olive trees. The road followed the river Guadalquiver, which, although now a narrow stream, is rapid, and had destroyed several parts of the road during the winter floods. A few miles after this we left the river side and ascended a chain of hills, near the summit of which we passed through a singular tunnel in the rock, called the Puerta reale, and entered the plain of Granada, through which we passed, and arrived there at three o'clock in the morning after a thirteen hours' drive. We and our carpet-bags were set down at the door of the post-office, where there was only one sleepy man to be seen, who took the mail-bags, and locked them up in a small office close to the door. He said he had no place for us even to sit down and wait in until daylight, and that we must go on to some hotel and try our luck there. We hesitated to walk through the narrow streets of the town, which after dark have not a good reputation for the honesty of their inhabitants. After a long talk, the man agreed to wake up a stout boy in an adjoining room, and when he arrived, we told him to shoulder our carpet-bags and show us the way to the hotel. It was pitch dark, and we had some difficulty in keeping close to our guide, as we tripped every moment over the rough pavement and other obstacles that the boy was more accustomed to steer his way through than we were. At last we arrived, and found all locked up; we knocked, and threw pebbles up at the windows till we roused a waiter, who put his head through a grating and told us our friends were not there. We now concluded they must be at the small hotel near the Alhambra, a mile and a half distant, and as we were very anxious to join them, we agreed to walk on there; but as the avenues leading up to it were so dark, we were afraid to venture without a light. At this juncture a watchman with a lantern in his hand appeared a little distance off. We hailed him, and he agreed

A NIGHT ARRIVAL.

to take care of us and deliver us up in safety at the Hotel de Ortiz, close to the towers of the Alhambra. We proceeded now without any fear of being robbed or stabbed, and we soon found ourselves at the door of our looked-for resting place. We woke up the landlady, who told us our friends were there, but fast asleep. She took us into a tidy room and got us some hot water. We made some tea, after which we lay down on the sofas in the room till breakfast-time, when we joined our friends.

CHAPTER V.

We have already described Granada; so we proceed with the narrative of a journey on mules across the country to Cordova. Some English friends had arranged to hire mules and ride by Alcalá la Real and Baena to Cordova, and from thence proceed by railway to Seville and Cadiz; and as we were now anxious to join the rest of our party whom we expected to leave Gibraltar and meet us at Cadiz, we were easily induced to join. By the assistance of Bensaken, a respectable guide who resides at Granada, and who speaks English, we engaged mules for the journey. We paid four dollars for each mule, and the same for the baggage mule. They were sorry animals, and we would willingly have paid more for good mules; indeed, but for this circumstance, we should have enjoyed our ride exceedingly. As our expedition was to take four days, and we knew that we should not find any luxuries, or even comforts, at the poor mountain posadas, we laid in a store of tea, sugar, chocolate, chickens, and ham; an apparatus for boiling water and making tea at any moment, with a spirit-of-wine lamp, as fires are seldom seen in Spain; also a kettle, a very necessary article if you wish to avoid the taste of oil and garlic. Sketch-books, guide-books, and an assortment of clothing, were packed in a large waterproof bag, made in the form of a huge purse; this was hung across the mule's back, and hung down on either side. Our side-saddles were peculiar, and not comfortable; they were a singular invention, like a camp stool with arms, placed upon the mule's back, the legs being fastened with ropes on to the girths; the upper part of the stool stood high above the mule's back, and formed a sort of arm-chair, upon which we sat sideways on a manta (or plaid) folded up into a square cushion; our feet were supported by a square of wood, hung like a shelf from the stool. We had no power of guiding our mules, which were all tied to each other, and followed in a string.

Our first day's journey was a short ride to Pinos, only ten miles from Granada. We passed through the irrigated plain, and all went merrily till we came to a deep, clay, muddy road, when our baggage mule fell, and could not be raised till he was relieved of the weight on his back, when our muleteer and some friendly passers-by tugged at his head and tail till we thought both would come off under their hands. When they at last succeeded in getting him on his legs, and had replaced the luggage, on we went, our muleteer singing and smoking as if nothing had happened, till we reached Pinos. It was here that Columbus was overtaken by Queen Isabella's messengers, and returned with them to receive his orders for his voyage of discovery. The bridge, before entering the town, is pretty; but as we arrived by moonlight, not having left Granada till the afternoon, it was too dark to see much of the surrounding country.

On arriving at the door of the posada, we entered its large open doors, and dismounted amongst packages, mules, and muleteers. Stumbling over mules' furniture and bales of goods, we made our way to the kitchen, in the centre of which a party of muleteers were sitting round a wood fire on the pavement, upon which simmered a large caldron, emitting a savoury odour. The majo of the party was playing on a guitar, the rest singing an accompaniment, and taking it in turn to stir the contents of the caldron. They regarded us with some astonishment, and, after much gesticulation, the majo, who proved to be the landlord, showed us into a small room opening out of the kitchen, containing a very doubtful-looking bed, a few ricketty chairs, and a table. We were prepared not to be easily discouraged, and asked for dinner in a confident sort of tone. We were told we should have a delicious fowl and *sopa*. The table was arranged to be ready for the expected dinner, a towel serving for a table-cloth, and the party assembled round it, but no sopa, no fowl, arrived. Many excursions were made to ask after its progress; the answer was, it was still "muy duro" (very hard). There was no resource but to return to our seats, and wait as patiently as we could. Our host evidently pitied our condition, and came in with a guitar in his hand; he sat down on one of the rickety chairs, and began to play wonderful airs and marches with great energy, executing most difficult shakes and trills. He was bent on soothing our savage appetites by sweet music. We took it kindly, but at last human nature could stand it no longer. "Make haste, we are very hungry," burst from our lips, extending our hands towards the door of the kitchen containing our long-looked-for fowl. It came at last; but having been boiled in a narrow-mouthed jar, into which it had been thrust with some difficulty, and being now considerably swollen, it baffled our ingenuity to extract it. Each of us tried successively to accomplish the feat without success, till, by the united efforts of our several forks, it was extricated, and placed upon a dish with its legs much extended. We then poured the soup into our plates, the only merit of which was its being hot, for it had nothing else to recommend it. The fowl still retained its character of *muy duro*, so we were obliged to have recourse to our own provision basket and tea-kettle.

In some of the rooms there was no glass, only shutters, to exclude the external air. One of our party thought that she had secured her door by locking it, and retired with an assurance of safety to rest on the bed as best she could. In the morning she tried to unlock her door; it was "muy duro" too. After much knocking and calling for assistance, the knight of the guitar came. After giving innumerable directions as to how she might open it, all which proved totally unsuccessful, he put his hand into a hole near the lock outside, and in one moment open it came. So much for the safety of a lock in a Spanish posada.

After partaking of a cup of chocolate and a roll of excellent bread, we prepared to start. It was still twilight when we mounted our mules, and followed a mule-path which wound up the Elora hills, which are bare, with only here and there tufts of aromatic shrubs. From the heights we looked down upon the Duke of Wellington's property of Soto de Roma. It has the appearance of being a fertile, highly cultivated, and extensive farm, very much irrigated. The house, a large farm-like-looking mansion, stands in the midst of olive groves, overlooking the plain to the south. A ride of five hours brought us to a wayside posada, where our mules were rested under cover of a large open shed, and ourselves refreshed with the provisions we had carried with us in our knapsacks. After this the country was stony and rugged. Here and there a lone ruined tower looked down upon us from conical bare grey hills. Soon after we ascended a very steep mountain side. Looking back towards Granada, we had a magnificent view of the Sierra-Nevada through a gorge of the Elvira hills. The sun was setting, and tinged the snowy summits with a glow of crimson light, which gradually faded to a pale purple, and the evening shadows reached us long before we reached the Moorish town of Alcala la Real, which stands high above the valley on a rock. The accommodation at this place was much the same as that of the preceding night.

The following morning we had to start early, as the distance to Baena was great, and there was no resting-place between these two towns. We again took our chocolate and bread before mounting our sorry steeds, and started at 5 o'clock A.M. The morning was chilly and frosty; the moon soon after set in the west, and the sun rose in the east, each giving a rosy glow of light. On we went for six hours, only varied by occasionally walking on foot a few miles when the road was good. A party of muleteers, with their long strings of mules, joined us. One of the muleteers was an intelligent and amusing man, full of information about his own country. He could not understand for what reason we **were** travelling through this part of the world; merely doing so for pleasure was to him perfectly unaccountable. He was anxious to know all our movements; where England was, and how we expected ever to return to it again. He also expressed a great desire to know our opinion of Spain, and his countrymen, and **if** we did not admire both very much.

The country here is entirely under corn crops, here and there a cork-tree dropped about the ground, like straggling trees in an English park. This district is monotonous and uninteresting, particularly in the winter months. We were credibly informed that in this country, where there are no inhabitants, or very few, the people come from various distant towns and mountain villages, till the soil, sow the seed, watch and protect the crop till reaped, and return with it to their homes.

After a seven hours' ride, we rested by the **side** of a well in patriarchal style. On approaching Baena, the country became much more interesting; several mountain villages crowned the heights of the hills around the fertile valley—corn, olives, and the locust-tree covering the land. During the last league of our journey, we were accompanied by dozens of peasants returning from their labour to the town, where they all lived. They were a fine, handsome people, cheerful and happy-looking, and they were extremely polite to us. The women's dress was very gay in colour—yellow and blue predominating in their dresses and handkerchiefs. The men were mostly attired in a brown suit of substantial-looking cloth and a bright scarlet sash, with handkerchief of some gaudy hue round their necks. There are no roads in this country: even where they have begun to make one out of a town, it only extends a mile or two, and suddenly ends in a hole; the intermediate distance between the towns are merely straggling paths. The bright idea of joining the two ends of the roads never seems to have entered into their heads as a means of facilitating traffic and increasing wealth.

Baena is a considerable town, and has once been of great importance, as may be seen by the remains of a square Moorish tower and a large dilapidated church. We were very thankful to reach Baena after a twelve hours' ride. The evening was cold, but during the day the sun was very overpowering, even in January: later on in the season the heat must be intolerable in the middle of the day.

The following morning at five we again started. In descending to the open vault-like stable to mount our mules, we stumbled over what appeared to us bundles of mantas lying in the doorways and under archways. These turned out to be muleteers, who had passed the night there, and who had not finished their night's rest. One occasionally woke up and procceded with his morning toilet, regardless of our presence. After many difficulties in arranging and balancing ourselves and our luggage on our uncomfortable saddles, we started, and again passed through corn-lands that looked as if the produce would feed half the population of Spain, if they had means of exporting it otherwise than in sacks on mules' backs across these interminable hills. The country became deep clay and mud as we reached and forded a small tributary to the river Guadalquiver. Fortunately the weather had been

H

fine, and the stream was not strong; even as it was, the water reached the girths of our mules. We wound round low hills till we reached the Guadalquiver,—here a wide, deep, muddy stream, its banks edged by willows and tamarisk; in many places it was much overflowed, and we had to take a higher path to avoid the banks of mud left by the great flood in the end of December.

We had been many hours on our saddles before we came to a welcome spring of water, and we gladly dismounted and unpacked our provisions of cold chicken, ham, and eggs, &c.; after which refreshment we spread out our mantas on the short sweet grass, and some of the party pleaded guilty to losing all sense of fatigue by taking a good sleep.

This is a great country for rearing horses on the extensive and undulating hills covered with short herbage. At distances of two or three miles are high-roofed sheds to protect and shelter the droves of horses from sun or rain. After this, the path descended to the muddy banks of the Guadalquiver. We ploughed and plunged through this sea of mud for leagues, our mules constantly stumbling and floundering. At seven o'clock in the evening we reached the ferry opposite Cordova, and crossed the river by a swinging-boat, made fast by a rope higher up the stream, and continued our course through gigantic aloes to the town of Cordova, which we reached at half-past eight o'clock, after being on the saddle fourteen hours.

After visiting the cathedral next day, we proceeded by rail to Seville. Here we heard that the rest of our party had found Gibraltar so agreeable and comfortable a residence, that they wished us to rejoin them there; we shall, consequently, defer our description of Seville until we have conducted our friends there also.

This winter was peculiar in respect to the number and extent of disastrous floods with which Spain was visited; it was thought more prudent, in consequence of this, to defer starting for Seville until March the 10th. Our sojourn at Gibraltar had been most agreeable. After a visit of two months, we left it with regret. The climate, coupled with the sanitary condition of the Rock, renders it perhaps superior to any other winter residence in Europe. The advantages of church, good medical advice, and the extensive garrison library, to which strangers are easily admitted as members, are not to be overlooked. We fortunately had taken letters of introduction to those highest in authority, from whom we met with the greatest kindness and attention; and we sympathised most heartily in the universal esteem and regard in which the present gallant governor and his estimable family are held by all ranks.

On the morning of the 11th of March we embarked for Cadiz in a large and powerful English steamer, which trades between the Mediterranean and London. Having had dire experience of Spanish steamers, we were greatly delighted with our sensible, upright, and straightforward captain, and indeed all his crew, who partook of the same character; and for the first time this winter we were at sea without any misgivings or fears of a change of weather. Provisions of all sorts were abundant and excellent on board, included in a very moderate fare.

The voyage occupied eight hours. Here, as at all ports in Spain, a small boat is necessary in landing and embarking. A short time sufficed to pass our effects through the custom-house; and our luggage was carried on men's shoulders half a mile to the hotel. The Blanco, said to be the best, being full, we were obliged to go to another, which was very second-rate. Here we remained over Sunday, and went to the English consul's house at 11 o'clock A.M., when he read prayers and an excellent sermon in a very appropriate way. There were not more than a dozen persons besides ourselves present. In the evening we walked to the church of los Capuchinos to see Murillo's picture of the marriage of St Catherine. It is of great size. It was while painting this picture from the top of a ladder that Murillo fell, and was so seriously injured that he died a few days after in consequence of it. The town stands on a promontory, and you look out to sea in all directions from it. There is very little to interest a stranger at Cadiz, and it is not thought as salubrious as many other places on the coast, which may be attributed to the bad drainage.

The following morning we went to Xeres in three hours by rail. The country, during the first part of the journey, is flat and low, with many districts of pasture and common land, upon which are fed droves of cattle and horses, and which are particularly favourable for rearing the latter. Towards Xeres there is only a small proportion of the country under vineyards, and a great part under corn, so that there is ample room to increase the existing quantity of vineyards. We took letters of introduction to the two largest establishments in the wine trade, and met with the greatest possible civility and attention from both. We tasted innumerable varieties of wine, some eighty, some one hundred and twenty, and some one hundred and forty years old, and every variety of *Pajarete* and other delicious wines. In one cellar or *bodiga*, we saw 14,000 butts of sherry. These bodigas are above ground, and have a free current of air through them; the casks are ranged in rows like streets, pilled one row above another, and stand generally three rows deep.

There is a tolerable hotel at Xeres, the Victoria; nothing can be more interesting than to spend a day there. Wine of first-rate quality can be bought at about £60 a butt, or £15 the quarter cask; this, with the addition of duty and freight, will come to about 30s. the dozen, or

£1 less than that usually charged for the same wine in England. From the lucrative nature of the wine trade, large quantities of wine are now being brought down by rail from the interior of Spain, to be turned into sherry for the English market. These are not inferior wines, and will increase the supply of second-rate wine, and prevent a rise in the price of the best wines. There is a very fine wine raised near Cordova, called Montilla. Extensive vineyards have lately been purchased here by one of the first houses in Xeres. Montilla is a very much esteemed and rather costly wine in Spain: a very first-rate butt is said to be worth £100. We were told that a certain Mr Holdsworth, a wine merchant in London, can supply some of the best of this wine. We mentioned Priorata as an excellent wine at Barcelona. At Malaga a good deal of wine is made exactly on the same principle as at Xeres, called dry Malaga. It is rather strong and hot, which arises from the greater amount of fermentation it undergoes in order to throw off the natural sweetness, and this fermentation is said to turn the sugar into alcohol; it is branded "Xeres," is called "Malaga Sherry," and costs £24 a butt. It is much used in adulterating sherry in England. "White Sweet Malaga" is the natural wine of the country, neither over fermented on the one hand, nor sweetened with boiled fruit and burnt sugar on the other, as of old. It is a good wholesome wine, is much used in the Spanish hospitals, and is approved of by those who like sweet wine; it is also good for culinary purposes. The price is £24 a butt, or £6 a quarter cask, which with duty would come to about 19s. a dozen in England. There is a still more delicate and delicious sweet wine to be got here, called "White Sweet Lucena;" the price is £7 the quarter cask. At Seville we were introduced to a certain intelligent Spanish duke, who told us that although there were many excellent wines in Spain, he thought that first-rate sherry was the best, and most adapted to the English taste. It is a curious fact, of which we were assured both at Xeres and Malaga, that the vegetable matter in wine retains a sort of life in it for about ten years; the wine regularly thickens every spring at the time the sap rises in the wine, and there is a corresponding change again in autumn.

We may conclude with a few remarks upon

port wine. Although we did not visit Oporto, yet in calling there in our passage by a Peninsular and Oriental steamer, we were fortunate enough to take on board a most agreeable fellow-passenger, who proved to be one of the first wine-merchants in Oporto. From him we learned that port wine of first-rate quality could be bought in Oporto for from £60 to £70 a pipe; that as the pipe runs five dozen more than a butt of sherry, port wine is quite as cheap as sherry. When we talked to him of the enormous prices that were charged by the English wine-merchants, he said, he was quite aware of that, for he had lately talked to one of his customers on the subject, who excused himself by telling him that not long since (no doubt ashamed of his enormous profits) he had written to a certain nobleman to offer him wine at a very considerable reduction in price, and received an answer stating that his lordship liked to be sure of what he drank, and he preferred paying the former high price.

CHAPTER VI.

THREE hours by rail from Xeres brought us to the great city of Seville. In many respects it has the advantage of Madrid, more particularly in climate. It is the residence of many old families and wealthy nobles and merchants; perhaps the second city of no country in Europe excels it. On a fine evening, and most evenings are fine here in March and April, there appear to be from one hundred and fifty to two hundred handsome carriages on the drive near the river Guadalquiver. The town is handsome and clean. In some parts it is ill-paved. The houses are commodious, with fine balconies and beautiful patios. They generally have an entrance-porch which leads to an open-worked iron gate, often very handsome. The interiors are built with open square courtyards or patios, on each side of which are corridors, supported by marble pillars. These patios are generally paved with black and white marble, and have fountains playing in the centre, around which flowers in porcelain vases are arranged. During the hot summer months, the family usually descend to the suite of apartments on the ground floor opening on to the patio, which they fit up and use as a drawing-room, and ascend to the upper suite of rooms on the first floor for the cold months of winter. Many of the houses are richly decorated with Moorish porcelain tiles, still called in the shops, where they imitate them very correctly, azulejos. The population of the town are well-clad, and apparently well-fed, and there is scarcely any appearance of poverty even among the lower ranks. The beggars, instead of being in rags, as at Naples, are almost always clean and well-clad, and are very often seen smoking a cigar.

The cathedral is one of the grandest in Europe. It is in beautiful repair, although it has been built many centuries; it could not be in a more perfect state if it had been erected only a few years since. The height of the nave and transepts is truly grand. The painted glass is beautiful, and there are some of Murillo's finest pictures in it, as well as others of the old Spanish school. Outside the cathedral in the Patio de los Naranjos, or court of the orange trees, is the Giralda, a Moorish tower and belfry. It is unique and exquisitely beautiful. It is 350 feet high; the upper 100 feet forming the belfry, was added in 1568. The view from the belfry is extensive. It is ascended with ease by 36 ramps, or paved slopes, instead of steps. Not far distant from the cathedral is the Louja, or town-hall, and the archbishop's palace.

Nearer the Moorish halls of the city, stands the Alcazar, or Royal Palace. It is, like all Moorish buildings, of plain exterior, but the interior is gorgeous with marble pillars, arches, arabesque tracery, courts, and corridors. The doors and ceilings are of inlaid wood, and are richly gilded; the walls and floors are in mosaic of coloured porcelain tiles, the patterns of which are geometrical, most varied and beautiful. The hall of the ambassadors is gorgeous with gilding. The grand patio is very similar to the court of Lions at the Alhambra. The whole has been restored within the last ten years; it is in perfect order, but the new colouring is too gaudy. The gardens laid out by Charles V. are more curious than beautiful. The Moorish bath, with its many gushing streams, is interesting; also the garden walks, through which pipes are laid from the fountains, and the unwary passer-by is suddenly surrounded by small jets of water playing round him from an unseen hand. The Alcazar contains a fine suite of rooms; for some time it was supposed that the King of Naples was to occupy them.

The Infanta and her husband, the Duke de Montpensier, have a handsome palace here, lately refitted and repaired. It has an extensive garden, teeming with oranges and flowering shrubs; also a fancy dairy, and zoological garden attached to it. In the museum, there is a chamber set apart for Murillo's pictures, where are to be seen twenty-four of his largest and best works; they are justly prized and considered of inestimable value.

At the Caridad (a convent and hospital for aged men) there are some of Murillo's celebrated pictures. At the church of the university there are some good pictures by Roelas; one small picture over the altar, of the Infant Saviour, is a most exquisite gem. All these beautiful pictures are separately and well described in Murray's handbook of Spain.

There is a residence of the Duke de Medina Celi, a cousin of the reigning family, called La Casade Pilatos, or Pilate's House, built completely after the Moorish fashion, and said to be an imitation of Pilate's house. It is very handsome, and there is a fine stair-case and gallery in it. There are also many other most interesting Moorish houses throughout the town.

There is an enormous cigar and tobacco manufactory, employing several thousand persons. It is a government monopoly, and is very similar to the one we described at Valencia. We visited the government establishment for making rifled cannon, and saw some good machinery; it was all stamped with the name of English makers. We were told it was small compared with English factories, yet we thought it very respectable.

There is an extensive parade-ground not far distant from the city. The Spanish troops are well clad, and they are active light men taken from the peasantry, from whom good material might be expected; but it is generally believed in Europe, that from a bad morale extending from

FOUNDLING HOSPITAL. 127

the highest to the lowest grades, although great boasters, their power of rapid marching is perhaps the only virtue they possess, and they are famous for making that most difficult exploit in war, a good retreat.

We visited a *Cuna*, or foundling hospital. It was necessary to give notice of our intended visit; so, perhaps, they were prepared for us. The house was beautifully clean. It was presided over by sisters of charity, who were neatly dressed, and appeared very kind to the children. In the first nursery there were thirty-three infants not exceeding three weeks old. They squalled very like those of Valencia. The sisters carried off the most noisy to the wet nurses. There is said to be a great mortality amongst them. A great many of these poor creatures suffer from delicate eyes; some had one, and some both eyes affected. We asked what was the usual treatment for these cases, and we were told they invariably bled for it. Bleeding is still the Spanish nostrum for all maladies.

In the train between Seville and Cordova, we met a gentleman who told us the following story: He is acquainted with a young lady in Madrid about twenty years of age, who is one of the most beautiful women in that great city. She is living under the protection of her reputed uncle and aunt, who are honest good people, and with whom she has resided since she was five years of age. She was impressed with the idea that she was not the child of her supposed father and mother, with whom she lived previously in a village near Seville, and latterly she had become most anxious to ascertain the true facts of her birth and parentage. Hearing that this gentleman was leaving Madrid to take a government office in Seville, she requested him to make minute inquiries. He visited the supposed mother, who was still residing in the same village, and told her of the suspicions of her reputed daughter, and implored her to state the truth. She at first assured him that the young lady was her own daughter, but upon his threatening her with punishment if she concealed the true facts, she confessed she had taken the child from the foundling hospital to bring it up as her own, a common act of benevolence amongst Spaniards; that she was instigated to do this by a young lady of high rank; and that she had received money for doing so. The lady had come several times to see the child, and each time had given her money. When the child was five years of age, an uncle and aunt of the woman were going to leave the country and settle at Madrid. They were pleased with the beauty of the little girl, and, having no children of their own, agreed to take her with them and to bring her up. The supposed mother not continuing very fond of the girl, and not finding her so good a bargain as she expected, readily gave her up. When next the real mother inquired for the child she told her it was dead. The gentleman then went to the foundling hospital to get what information he could from the Sisters of Charity there. With infinite trouble and difficulty he at length traced both the father and mother. They were both unmarried at the time of the birth of the child, and they are of the most distinguished families of Seville, and very rich. Now they are married, but not to each other, therefore they can never acknowledge their daughter. The mother had remained unmarried as long as she believed her child to be alive, but now they both know the whole story. The gentleman who told us this story manifested the greatest feeling and interest in it—so much so, that we could have no doubt of its truth. He also appeared rather a character. He told us the bull-fight was his ruling passion, and that at a great amateur bull-fight at Alicante, for a charitable purpose, he had acted as one of the principal chulos in the arena.

The country around Seville is very flat, and much overflowed in the winter time; but the climate is charming in March and April: in summer it is excessively hot. There is one large square in Seville, with rows of fine orange-trees around it. It is not long since this square was formed. It is a favourite resort towards evening. Ladies are not so often seen on foot here as in other Spanish towns. They still retain many Moorish customs in their houses, where they make a drawing-room of the patios and corridors, and spend much of their time in reclining on ottomans and eating bonbons. They invariably wear a mantilla or veil of black lace, velvet, silk, or gauze, which is pinned on the back of the head at each side, and flows over the shoulders for about a yard on either side. The black lace mantillas are very beautiful, and some of them of very great value. They do not consider their

BULL-FIGHT COSTUMES.

toilette complete if they have not a fan in their hands; indeed, they are so accustomed to its constant use that they even fan themselves in bed.

The hotels are tolerable: the Hotel de Paris is the best. The shops in Seville are not showy, but most articles of necessity or luxury can be found in them.

As in other large towns in Spain, each street is devoted to a particular trade. It is well worth making a visit to the tailors who make the gorgeous dresses for the matadors and picadors at the bull-fights. We saw about thirty men and women at work embroidering the rich velvet cloaks, jackets, waistcoats, &c., with gold and silver braid and spangles. The suit is usually made of one colour, either crimson, pale sea-green, violet, scarlet, blue, or mauve, according to taste. The short jackets are completely covered with gold and silver braid, spangles, silver buttons, and silk tassels. A very handsome jacket costs about £30. The cloak is in the form of a bornous, and is edged or spotted over with gold or silver spangles. The waistcoat is equally gorgeous, The faja worn round the waist is of the finest spun silk, the ends heavily embroidered. The knee-breeches are made of woven elastic silk, and have a wide piece of embroidery sewed down the outside of the legs, and are finished off at the knees with a large bow of ribbon. The matadors wear white silk stockings and polished black leather pumps, with buckles or a large bow of ribbon. On their heads they wear the invariable little round black velvet hat, with a large flower placed jauntily at one side of it. Their hair, which they usually wear long, is tied up in a roll at the back of their heads, and fastened with a large bow of some bright-coloured ribbon. A full suit for a bull-fight costs from £100 to £120.

We visited a corral or lodging-house for the lower classes. The house was formerly a nobleman's palace, and it is now let out in separate apartments. There was a large patio in the centre, and an open corridor both around the ground floor and the first story. There was a large fountain with a copious supply of water in the middle of the patio. All the apartments open into the corridors, and there were sixty separate families living in these; but there being no kitchen, they each had a separate little square furnace, about three feet high, placed alongside the pillar that supported the roof of the corridor. We paid our visit here at the dinner hour: they were mostly occupied cooking their repasts. The usual dish was *sopa* or soup; one civil woman told us how it was prepared. The receipt for it was, a tea-cupful of boiling water put into a bowl, to which was added some oil and garlic: upon the top of this is placed sufficient sliced bread to absorb the whole of the contents of the bowl, which is then turned out into a plate, and looks much more like a pudding than soup. These families, being accustomed to congregate together, live very harmoniously, and they looked cheerful and happy.

We afterwards went to the Corral del Conde, or washing establishment, where three hundred women were employed. The building is a large square court. There is an enormous fountain in the centre, surrounded by square stone troughs at which the women were busily washing. There were ropes extended from side to side of the court, and these were covered with linen and garments of every hue, shape, and colour, under the process of drying. This is not considered so respectable an establishment as the first corral we visited.

A few days previous to the holy week a party of men were occupied in erecting an enormous wooden temple or monument in the cathedral near the principal entrance. It is painted in imitation of white marble, ornamented with gilding. In the centre of this monument is a *custodia*, in which the host is deposited and the holy oil placed on Holy Thursday, after which it is brilliantly lighted up with innumerable wax lights. This monument is in exceedingly bad taste and quite out of character with the fine architecture of the cathedral.

On Palm Sunday we went to the cathedral at 8 A.M. to see the palm leaves and olive branches blessed. The cardinal bishop, a feeble old man, with a gentle expression of face, and his clergy in rich vestments, were performing high mass, after which they blessed the palm leaves and olive branches, and descended the steps of the altar in procession, some carrying palm leaves much decorated with gold in their hands; others of the clergy distributed the palm leaves and olive branches to the crowd. The Infanta and her husband the Duke of Montpensier, their daughter, and nephew (a son of the Duke of Nemours) and their suite, who had attended high mass, followed in the procession. They all passed out of the cathedral by the west door, and re-entered it at the east door when they returned to the high altar. There the bishop was divested of his mitre and robes; after which he was assisted down the steps of the altar, and he retired blessing the crowd. His countenance was most amiable and kind, and the crowd seemed to have great respect and reverence for him. The Infanta and her party remained to hear a sermon by a celebrated preacher.

At five o'clock the same day we went to a balcony in a street leading to the cathedral, where the processions of the holy week were to pass, and which we had hired for the week at a cost of £2, 10s. A dais was prepared for the Infanta at the town-hall, in the Plaza Francesco. Soon after five o'clock a procession appeared at the end of the street, moving onwards to the cathedral. It consisted of *white penitents,* who were fifty men in grotesque dresses of white cotton with yellow sashes round the waists, and a long white scarf over a pointed sugar-loaf hat which completely concealed their faces, only two small holes being cut for the eyes, and to enable them to see their way. Each penitent carried a lighted taper in his hand. Gentlemen consider it an honour to be allowed to attend the processions in this guise. After these penitents followed a paso or platform about fourteen feet long and eight feet wide ; a deep fringe or curtain is fastened round it, and above it is a handsome canopy of coloured silk, and gold and silver fringes, supported by silver or brass pillars. The images, rather larger than life, are placed upon it, and many wax tapers lighted round the images and in front of them. This paso, which is of great weight, is carried on the shoulders of twenty-four Gallician porters, here called Gallegos. These men are usually hewers of wood and water-carriers. On the first platform or paso was a wooden image representing our Saviour bound before Pontius Pilate, and guarded by six Roman soldiers. This paso was preceded by a military band, and followed by several men dressed in Roman attire. The next procession was preceded by black penitents, the dress of these men being similar to the white penitents previously described, except in colour.

The next paso carried a very large and beautifully carved image of the Virgin. The dress of this was of very rich white satin and gold; the mantle suspended from the shoulders was of black velvet, very full, wide, and flowing, and richly embroidered with gold. The arms, neck, and bosom of the image were covered with jewels. The expression of the face was very sweet and melancholy; but much of its beauty destroyed by its being so highly varnished. An image of St John was placed on the same platform behind that of the Virgin. This paso was attended by detachments of military and bands of music. The third paso represented our Saviour's triumphal entry into Jerusalem riding on an ass. The ass was a very large specimen, stuffed; and the whole was overshadowed by a palm-tree, in the branches of which was a diminutive figure in a white cotton dress, and a large straw hat and blue feathers, representing Zaccheus. The fourth paso carried an image of the Virgin alone, with a flowing white lace dress, a magnificent dagger set with diamonds on her breast; the mantle of dark blue velvet, five or six yards long and many yards wide. This was hung from the neck of the image, and was so long that it hung over the platform, and was supported by two little boys in white and blue dresses. The fifth and last paso of this day, was a crucifixion, not only of our Saviour but also of the two thieves. These images are kept in the different churches; and we were told that all the images of the Virgin Mary have maids of honour chosen from the ladies of the noblest families or first citizens, and these have the charge of their valuable robes and jewels, and their office is to dress the images for these processions. We were told that these pasos had a very considerable effect in reviving religious feeling annually amongst the Spaniards; but we apprehend that, as in American or Scotch revivals, there is more of fanaticism than religion, and that the good effect is not very lasting.

On Wednesday of the Holy Week is the ceremony of the rending of the white veil in the cathedral, which is not so impressive as the rending of the black veil on the following Saturday. On the 28th of March (Holy Thursday) we

HOLY THURSDAY.

attended the service of the benediction of the oil to be used for extreme unction and other ceremonies during the ensuing year. The service took place in the sacristia of the cathedral. The cardinal, bishop, and fifty priests were present. On this day the beautiful agate doors of the custodia above the altar are opened, and the valuable relics it contains exhibited. In the centre of the **chapel a** long table was placed, upon which stood **two** gold vases about two feet high. After several prayers were said, and the ceremony of the benediction of the oil in golden cups upon the altar was over, the priests walked with these cups in their hands, and poured the consecrated oil into the two vases on the table, after which they took the vases on golden trays, and all the priests followed in procession and conveyed them to the high altar, where the Infanta and her suite, as on Palm Sunday, were already seated on a crimson **velvet** dais at one side of the altar. High mass was performed, after which the procession again formed, and the priests carried the host and the consecrated **oil to** the custodia in the white monument, followed by the Infanta and her suite. On this occasion the Infanta and her daughter, who is about thirteen years of age, wore full court-dresses and trains; the former wore a white silk dress, and a pale pink brocaded silk train, trimmed with white Brussels lace, a tiara and necklace of diamonds and pearls, and a white lace mantilla. The princess, her daughter, wore a white silk dress and a blue train, and a wreath of pink roses. The younger members of the family wore blue and white dresses. The Duke of Montpensier wore a rich military uniform; his nephew had blue and richer regimentals. The ladies of the suite wore full court-dress. The royal family followed the bishop and the clergy, each bearing a lighted taper in their hands, and, on arriving at the monument, they knelt upon the steps round it till the priests placed the host in the custodia, after which they separated. The Infanta and her suite walked to the door of the cathedral, where the carriages were waiting to convey them back to the palace, and the bishop and clergy went into the sacristia to unrobe. It is here that the wardrobes containing the priests' vestments are placed.

At 11 A.M. the same day a dinner was laid for twelve poor men in the bishop's palace, where the bishop was to serve them and give them his blessing. The crowd of respectable people making their way into the palace was immense, and it was with great difficulty we got entrance, with the assistance of some civil Spaniards, who, seeing we were strangers, assisted us. We entered one of the long galleries, and found twelve respectable-looking old men sitting at a table ready to begin their repast. We passed on, and made our exit into a patio at the opposite side of the palace from which we had entered it.

At three o'clock that afternoon we saw the ceremony of the bishop washing the feet of thirteen old men at the cathedral. These were dressed in a new suit of brown cloth, the donation of the bishop, and seated on benches placed on a platform raised between the high altar and the coro. Six men were placed at one side, and seven on the other; the thirteenth man has always been added to the original twelve since a miraculous thirteenth was discovered after the service many years ago. The bishop was placed on a throne in the centre of the platform. Each old man had a napkin thrown over his shoulder, and the shoe and stocking off the right foot.

After a long service of robing and unrobing the bishop, a sacristan entered with a golden ewer and basin. The bishop took them from the sacristan and went round the platform and washed, or rather poured water on, each man's foot, wiped it with the napkin placed on the man's shoulder, and kissed it. The bishop returned to his throne, and a priest entered the pulpit near, read some verses out of the Testament; and after doing so, preached a sermon most impressively, which the immense crowd listened to most attentively and respectfully.

At four o'clock that day, the Infanta and her party, in full court dress, visited the monument in the cathedral, and knelt down before the host in the custodia with great appearance of reverence and devotion; after which they left the cathedral on foot, and walked through the streets to their dais at the town-hall, to see the pasos come from their respective churches to the cathedral. We took our places, as formerly, in the balcony overlooking the street through which the processions were to pass. They were very similar to those we had seen on Palm Sunday, except three. One was an image of our Saviour praying in the garden of

THE MISERERE. 143

Gethsemane, Elias and Moses standing by his side, and St Peter and St John represented as sleeping; the second was our Saviour bearing his cross; the third a very finely carved image of Isaiah with the book of prophecies in his hand. This figure was of gigantic size. Before and after each of these pasos were cavalry and infantry in Roman attire.

At ten o'clock the same evening we went to the cathedral to hear the Miserere. This was the most solemn and impressive service of the holy week. The enormous cathedral was brilliantly lighted up, and, from its vast extent, there was a hazy and beautiful light throughout its numerous lofty and grand aisles. Groups of females, in black dresses and mantillas, were sitting or kneeling upon the marble pavement with perfect stillness and deep devotion in their attitudes; the male portion of worshippers were spread about in every direction, and all seemed devout. The music was soft and beautiful, and floated through the vast edifice. We were told the greater part of the people remained in the cathedral all night, to see two pasos and processions enter it soon after midnight, after which was high mass.

On Good Friday, at eight o'clock in the morning the great candelabra at the high altar was lighted, the only day of the year in which it is done. At five o'clock in the afternoon there were more processions and pasos. One of these was the entombment of our Saviour, and the three Maries represented as kneeling beside the grave; and another of the Virgin Mary, which was magnificently adorned with jewels and a splendid mantle of crimson velvet and gold. The following morning (Saturday), we went to the cathedral to witness the grand ceremony of the rending of the black veil which was hung behind the high altar. There was high mass. The cathedral was densely crowded, and all seemed in the greatest state of expectation, yet the greatest quietude prevailed. At the conclusion of the high mass a rifle was fired as a signal; simultaneously fireworks, which had been placed around the galleries and under the arches, were made to explode; this was accompanied by artificial thunder. We kept our eyes fixed on the black veil. In the midst of the roar of fireworks and thunder the veil was rent from the top to the bottom with a loud crash. The means taken to do this were not well concealed, as we could see the feet of the men who were pulling the cords at each side to cause the veil to be divided. Immediately after, the two fine organs pealed forth a grand burst of music, which continued some time, and they finished off with a modern waltz. Easter day is heralded in by a peal of bells at midnight. The services of this day are not very impressive or unusual, and the afternoon is devoted to the first great bull-fight of the season. On this occasion the Spaniards seem in the same excitement that the English are on the day of a great race. Thousands of people come into the town, and they are seen streaming towards it in every direction. There are also great bull-fights of equal magnificence at the fair, which takes place about the 18th of April, and lasts three days.

K

CHAPTER VII.

"Quien no ha vistoa Sevilla no ha visto maravilla" (he who has not seen Seville has not seen a wonder). This is true of Seville at all times, but more especially at the season of the annual fair. For some days previous, an immense concourse of strangers of every rank pours into the town. The prices of houses, lodgings, carriages, &c., are quadrupled. The masters of the herds of cattle and horses are splendidly mounted, and are seen accompanying their charges towards the fair, which is held on a very extensive plain on the immediate outskirts of the city. The immense flocks of horses, horned cattle, and sheep, much resemble those of some of our great annual cattle fairs in England. The street of tents for the nobles and rich people, has evidently had its origin in the necessity and advantage of their presence at the disposal of their flocks and herds, so that pleasure and fashion seem to have been wisely combined with profit. The nobles from Madrid, ladies in maja dresses (the old Spanish costume), peasants from the Sierra Morena in their varied costumes, Russian artists, English officers from Gibraltar, French engineers, German traders, American travellers, are all seen in motley groups.

Every family who can afford it has a tent at the fair, where they spend the whole day. These tents are made of a rough framework of wood, covered with canvass or striped cotton. Some of them contain a few chairs and mats; others are much ornamented with bright-coloured draperies and flags, and furnished with sofas, armchairs, tables, and grey-coloured mats, and quantities of flowers in porcelain vases, arranged with taste at the doors, and within the tents. They are generally divided into two parts: the servants occupy the apartment at the back, and are always in readiness to serve refreshments and cold water from the cool porous jars. All the world pay each other visits, when wine, fruits, sweetmeats, chocolate, and coffee, are offered to the guests. In the tents of the humbler class, nuts, a sort of sweet bean, bonbons, and cold water (the latter is a constant necessity with the Spaniards), are offered to their friends.

The most magnificent tents are those of the two great clubs, who, for the time, adjourn from their club-houses in the town to these tents in the fair. In the evening they have music and dancing, and they are much crowded with gaily-dressed ladies and gentlemen. There are other tents less aristocratic, where there is plenty of dancing, and in some there are comedians, so that the peasants may see a tolerable performance for a few pence. There are long streets of tents occupied by gypsies, and others have booths for the sale of knives, daggers, and toys. Between these rows of tents and booths all the gay world move in carriages or on foot; and, in the brilliant sunshine at this season, the scene is very animated. In the quarter where the cattle and horses are sold, the scene is lively and amusing. The herdsmen have their little fireplaces near their flocks, and are seen cooking their food. The horned cattle are fawn-coloured, but not fine as compared with English animals. The sheep are of large size: their wool is of very fine texture. The horses are well fed and handsome—generally of a stamp that would

BULL-FIGHTS.

bring about £100 in England, though we did not hear of any long prices being asked or given. From the badness of the roads almost all Spaniards ride, and seem more at home on horseback than anywhere else.

The gypsies are conspicuous at the fair, particularly the females, who are cleanly and prettily dressed in white muslin, which forms a striking contrast to their olive skins and black eyes. Many of these preside over small stalls, where they distribute a delicacy well known at Seville—the hot circular cakes called buñuelos.

Upon the first and last days of the fair are very grand bull-fights; they commence at four o'clock in the afternoon. The Infanta, in a rich maja dress, and the Duke of Montpensier, his family and suite, all attend it in full dress. In the surrounding benches were seated about 12,000 persons, both male and female, of every rank, in holiday attire. There were no clergy in full canonicals, as described by Mr Ford, but we were assured many were present in plain clothes. The arena is very large: the open space into which the bulls are admitted could not be less than a hundred yards in diameter. It is wrong to call this "Correda de Toros" a bull-fight; the poor bull has no more chance with his numerous assailants than a rat turned out to be worried. When knights of old, on gallant steeds, charged the bull lance in hand, it might with more propriety have been called a bull-fight; but when modern Spaniards sit, cigar in mouth, and watch a paid picador do the work, it will be easy to find a more appropriate translation of "Correda de Toros." The picadors or horsemen, the chulos or men on foot, with gay-coloured cloaks, and the matadors or killers, are dressed in gorgeous antique costume, and certainly have an imposing effect; but the poor bull, lately taken from his native pastures, in the prime of his youth and strength, being a four-year old, is roused, and made to rush into the middle of the arena; here he halts, and stares with bewilderment and surprise at the assembled thousands, who greet his arrival with clapping of hands.

The majority of these animals were black, though some were of a yellowish dun, not unlike some of our West Highlanders, with wide horns from one and a half to two feet long. They were wanting in the breadth of our favourite British breeds. From the middle of the arena the bull was soon provoked to make desperate charges, right and left, at chulos and picadors, the former showing the greatest activity in vaulting over the palisades, or escaping into the narrow side-niches, where the bull cannot follow. **The picadors receive** the charge of the bull by meeting him **with** the point of their lance, which is a short knife on the point of a pole about eight feet long. With this they meet or catch him on the shoulder, which always mitigates, and often completely checks, **his** charge. The bull sometimes avoids the lance, and it is then he gores **the horse, or** sends him and his rider sprawling in the dust. Cut and goaded with the lances **of** the picadors, and exhausted by fruitless charges at the gay cloaks of the chulos, he at last yields **to** the lords of the creation, and looks out for the entrance through which he had been admitted. Thus far the "Correda de Toros" was a fight; and here, were the poor bull, baffled and conquered, allowed to retire, a subdued animal, all would be well, and **in** harmony with English notions of **a** bull-fight, **and** of fair play; but now, when the poor bull is exhausted by his attacks on his antagonists, more than one of whose steeds is seen dead on the ground, and others, with their bowels protruding, are kept with difficulty on their legs, to receive further charges of the bull, a trumpet sounds, and more tormentors come forth in the shape of men, with barbed darts in their hands, called bandorilleros; these they fling with great dexterity and fasten in the bull's neck, till the agony completes his exhaustion, and the matador is now summoned by a second blast of the trumpet. He finally, after prolonged endeavours, succeeds in running a sword down between his shoulders to his heart, when the mighty beast falls, and is as harmless as a worm. The numbers of bulls killed at each correda is generally eight; and as soon as one is killed, he is rapidly removed by mules in gay trappings, who drag him off the arena by a noose fastened round the horns, and in five minutes a fresh bull comes snorting forward.

The Spanish say they love bull-fighting "because they are more brave than all other men;" but their bravery reminds one much of a certain little boy who said "he would like to look in at a gate and see a battle." The sport, if such it can be called, is cruel, and perhaps degrading; and it is possible that, with a more advanced state of civilisation, it would, like the less cruel sports of cock-fighting and bull-baiting in England, cease to find admirers.

Although out of date, it is perhaps not out of place here to describe a Portuguese bull-fight, which we afterwards witnessed at Lisbon.

The amphitheatre there is about one-half the size of that of Seville, but, being more closely seated, it holds a large number of spectators. On this occasion there might have been 10,000 persons present. The building is entirely of wood, and is a rough affair. The people seem enthusiastic in their appreciation of the sport. Thirteen bulls were advertised to be brought forward.

The amphitheatre was crowded half an hour before the opening of the ceremony; and, as in other countries, the boys, in what represents the pit in a theatre, are very impatient, and shout picador, &c., &c. All the actors, or those to be engaged in the sport, marched in procession at the appointed hour, a quarter before five o'clock in the evening. This procession consisted of four men on horseback, four chulos, eight men dressed in yellow buckskin breeches and red flannel shirt and caps, called forzadors, and two men who threw the barbed darts, called bandorilleros

—all these entered ceremoniously, and stood in as imposing order as possible. Then entered Don Basilio, the principal and celebrated horseman. He is a fine-looking man, of sixty years of age, and was dressed in a court suit and cocked hat. He was mounted on a fine powerful dark-brown horse, upon which he passaged and capered around the arena. He was received with repeated bursts of admiration, and bowed graciously to the assembled multitude. The Portuguese staff for the bull fight, although individually well dressed, was very inferior to that of Seville. The bull-fight also differs from that of Spain. In the first place, the bull, though sometimes roughly handled, is never put to death. When completely baffled, and too much beaten or exhausted to afford any more sport, a small herd of eight or ten work-oxen are driven into the arena, and he is readily induced to accompany them off the stage : and, secondly, the bull always has his horns muffled; in this state, the horns appear nearly as thick at the points as at the roots. We had observed that when an ox is being shod in Spain, he is driven into a narrow space between two walls, where a beam of wood is passed through in front of his chest, another behind his horns, and a third behind his tail; after which his leg is tied up, so that the farrier can perform with ease and safety. We doubt not but that by some such process the bull is muffled, and is rendered comparatively harmless. By this means the spectators are spared the revolting scenes of blood and gore and disembowelled horses; and as the bull is never put to death, a Portuguese bull-fight is a much less sanguinary affair than that of Spain.

From where we sat we had a view of the bulls as they were brought forward, ready for the opening of a small door to burst forth and meet their opponents. We saw that they were severely goaded, through a hole in the roof of this passage, to rouse them, and make them rush forward as soon as released. Only about one-third of the bulls were of large size, and all of them were black except one, which was brindled, and had a white face like a Herefordshire ox. The finest bulls were brought forward first. As soon as the bull rushed into the arena, the old man, Don Basilio, in a cocked-hat, white waistcoat, and jack-boots, lance in hand, on his magnificent horse, charged past him, and round him, on which the bull immediately showed fight, and rushed furiously after the horse, but was gallantly speared in the neck by the rider, and turned in his course. The bull then rushed at the nearest chulo; and, after several unsuccessful charges, was again met by the gallant Basilio, who broke half-a-dozen spears on his neck as the bull endeavoured to gore the horse. These charges of Don Basilio's exceeded in interest and excitement anything in the Spanish bull-fight, although, in respect of dress, the Spanish is the more gorgeous and imposing scene. The lance Don Basilio used on this occasion was about eight feet long. After he had fought this bull manfully, he retired, and only returned once again, on a different steed, to accomplish his greatest feat—namely, to plant a short spear of three feet long in the bull's neck.

The chulos and bandorilleros wore out and fatigued the rest of the bulls, and as each of these got exhausted, the forzadors, dressed in yellow buckskin and red caps, came forward courting a charge of the bull; and when any one could not conveniently escape, he threw himself between the bull's horns, hugging his neck, when his companions seized his horns, and the weight of three men on his head, two or three on his back, and one or two holding on by his tail, rendered the bull harmless. This taking the bull by the horns was altogether most ridiculous. Very frequently one of these men would drop on his knees right in front of the bull, and when the furious beast charged at him, he threw himself so flat on the ground that the bull charged over him. On one occasion the man was tossed, but not much injured; and he immediately made it a plea for going round with his cap and soliciting money from the spectators, who seemed to give freely. The last scene with each bull, previous to being driven out of the arena with the work-oxen, was his being overpowered by the forzadors.

The following is the description of another Spanish fête, from reliable information:—Once every year, at the fair at Puerto Santa Maria, near Cadiz, a savage bull is turned loose in the streets with a long cord fastened round his head and trailing along the ground. Whenever he rushes at a person, he makes his escape by jumping up on to one of the windows, which are a few feet from the ground: the crowd behind the bull then pull at the cord and turn him. A gentleman was following in the crowd last year, when the bull rushed down the street till it came to a cross-street. Here the chances were he would take one of the three roads in front of him ; but suddenly wheeling round, he rushed at the mob behind him, and tossed and killed one unfortunate man on the spot. Sickened at this sight, the gentleman left the scene of the disaster and retired to his hotel, only to be still more horrified by a Spaniard's coming in and coolly telling a friend what capital sport they had had,— how well the bull had behaved—that he had killed another man. This was considered quite an ordinary event, as one or two men at least are killed every year.

Those who leave Seville to proceed to Madrid pass through Cordova, but are obliged to take a through ticket by the railway and diligence, which allows them no time to stop at Cordova. It is impossible to see the wonderful cathedral without arranging to remain a few hours for that purpose. It might be advisable, after taking a through ticket to Madrid, to start by an earlier train, and so have an hour or two in advance at Cordova. For example, the diligence train starts at 2 P.M.

from Seville, and there is also a train at 8 A.M., which would allow some hours to see Cordova and dine before the diligence comes up.

There are five or six coaching companies between Seville, Cordova, and Madrid; some of them are said to be bad and ill-served. The Compañia del Norte y Mediodia is perhaps the most punctual and well-regulated, but the Cordovesa is also very good. Each company stops at different fondas in the large towns, but, as a general rule, the Norte y Mediodia stops at the best. The diligence leaves Cordova at 7 P.M., and arrives at Andujar at 9 A.M. the following morning. Passengers breakfast here, and proceed to Bailen, after which the road ascends the hills of the Sierra Morena to the town of Santa Catalina, which place is reached at half-past 3 P.M., and here passengers dine, and go on to Val de Peñas, arriving there in the middle of the night, and proceeding to Manzanares, where they arrive at 6 A.M. Here the diligence meets the railway for Madrid, which takes four hours more. The journey from Seville to Madrid occupies forty hours. At the station of Castillejo, on this line, is a branch railway to Toledo; but as the hotels are bad there, it is better to visit it from Madrid. It takes four hours by rail from that city to Toledo, and there are trains that will suit to take passengers back to Madrid in the evening.

Those who travel from Seville to Cadiz and return to England by steam, should not omit, before leaving Seville, to visit Cordova by rail. The fare is eleven shillings, and it is only a day's excursion to go by the morning train and return by that of the afternoon. There is, however, a very good hotel at Cordova—the Fonda Rezzi—the landlord of which is civil and obliging.

The cathedral is unique, and, in the words of an American traveller whom we met, "very queer indeed." It is an old Moorish mosque, very much in its original state ; there are innumerable horse-shoe arches, and 854 marble pillars, which support a low roof. This mosque was originally lighted, in the time of the Moors, by thousands of lamps which were kept burning day and night, and no sunlight was admitted. This must have had a very imposing effect. The Christians, however, upraised eight domes or cupolas, by which it is now lighted. The small chapel, which was originally the "shihrab," or sanctuary for the

THE GUADALQUIVIR. 161

Koran, is very magnificently ornamented with costly mosaics. As the Moorish pilgrims entered this sanctuary and passed round the Koran, which was suspended from the centre of the roof, they moved sideways, always keeping their faces towards the Koran. These pilgrims were so numerous that the multitudes who have passed round barefooted have worn a deep hollow in the marble pavement. There is a great deal that is most interesting in this wonderful mosque : the numerous pillars, all bearing different characters (and on some of which the carving is very singular), require some hours to examine and to see thoroughly.

There is a fine old Roman bridge across the Guadalquivir. It is far from being a grand city, but it is old and interesting, and there are the mansions of many aristocratic families in it; so much so, that the Spaniards say, "It is the most respectable city in Spain to be born in, though not the most agreeable to live in." The country between Seville and Cordova is in some places picturesque. The Guadalquivir, which has a name familiar in romance, is at this part of its course a muddy and uninteresting stream. Before leaving

L

Seville we ought to remark that the people seem generally loyal, and they respect and are sufficiently contented with their Queen and her government, and more particularly with the administration of affairs by her present Prime Minister, O'Donnel. We have mentioned that the Infanta (the Queen's sister), with her husband, the Duke of Montpensier, preside at the principal fêtes here. The people say the Infanta is more talented and estimable than her sister. The Infanta and her husband identify themselves much with the people, and are deservedly popular. Whether justly or not, the Queen-Mother Christina seems to have been made a scape-goat, and to have carried away with her all the disloyalty of the people, and the disreputable character of her court. We mentioned to a Spaniard that a place of honour had been reserved for her in Rome, by the side of the Pope. "Ah! well," replied she, "he may keep a place for her in Rome, but he cannot keep a place for her in heaven. When she dies she will go straight to the devil—I know that."

CHAPTER VIII.

We left Seville at 8 A.M., and arrived at Cadiz at half-past 12 o'clock. We had some difficulty in getting our passports signed in time to sail by the French steamer for Lisbon, which was to sail at 4 P.M. These steamers are small, but tolerably well appointed. The fares are exceedingly high—for this voyage of thirty-six hours we paid £3, 16s. for each ticket. We sailed up the river Tagus on a fine spring morning; the banks are undulating, green, and rather low; the prospect, on the whole, was English. On coming near the city of Lisbon, we found it a long straggling town, on the slope of a hill about 300 feet high. This is intersected by several valleys or ravines. Some of the buildings are large and massive. It is a fatiguing town to walk or drive through, on account of the continual ascents and descents. There are several public gardens throughout the town, none of which are large enough to be imposing. The city is completely defenceless from the sea, and quite at the mercy of a dominant maritime power. The Portuguese do not feel as kindly towards us as they ought to do, for our alliance and protection. They are very apt to say, "It is as convenient for England and her trade to extend this protection, as it is for us to receive it."

Before landing, we were visited by customhouse boats and sanitary officers, in all, fifty-three men, while, to the best of our knowledge, there was not fifty-three shillings' worth of cargo landed from our French steamer. We were told at another time that one of the evils and causes of the inefficiency of their customhouse proceeded from the number of officials; that where six active men could do the work well, and be well paid, Portuguese patronage was so valuable that they preferred dividing the emolument amongst forty inefficient officials.

We went to the Braganza Hotel, which is in a good situation, and, barring a few cockroaches, we were very comfortable. The bread in Portugal is very inferior to that of Spain; there are, however, several English luxuries to be met with here, on account of the shortness of the voyage to England.

There are still some vestiges of the dreadful earthquake. In the centre of the city is the ruin of a church destroyed at that fearful time. The roof is completely gone, and the walls, although standing, are in many places cracked. The gables still stand, with a part of the fine old windows, which are in a very shattered state. At one place there are evident marks of fire. There are still some blue and white porcelain tiles adhering to the walls. The cloisters are made into cavalry barracks; a Portuguese officer showed us through them. The horses were in good order, and there were some handsome animals amongst them. We saw the cloister-garden, which must once have been most productive, as there were the remains of a fine collection of fruit-trees; now it is much overgrown with shrubs. In one of the warm corners there was a very fine Japan medlar-tree covered with yellow fruit the size of a very large plum. We were presented with some, and we found the flavour very pleasant—a sharp refreshing acid.

In the Chapel of St Roque there are magnificent mosaics. The altar of this rich chapel is of amethyst and lapis lazuli. There are also eight columns of lapis lazuli. The three pictures in the finest mosaic are very beautiful, and resemble the most finished paintings. The one over the altar, of St John baptising our Saviour, is after Michael Angelo. At the sides of the chapel are the Annunciation, after Guido, in which the robe of the Virgin is of a singular and lovely purple; and the Descent from the Cross, after Raphael Urbino. The frames of these pictures are of a warm-coloured grey marble. Fifteen years were spent on these works of art. This chapel was placed, in 1744, in St Peter's at Rome. Benedict XIV. consecrated it, after which it was taken down and conveyed to Portugal by Don John V. in 1746, and placed in the Church of San Roque. There are two magnificent candelabra of bronze, and partly gilt; these stand on the step going up to the altar, one at each side. There are also three elegant lamps suspended from the roof of the chapel. The church is at present under repair, but there is not much to see in it.

Adjoining, and under the same roof, is the Cuna, or Foundling Hospital. It is not quite on the same principle as those at Seville and Valencia, in Spain. It is not only for foundlings, but for the children of parents who are unable to support them at home; at all events, they are allowed to take advantage of the charity. On the day on which we were there we saw eighteen women in a room set apart for the purpose, nursing their children for the last time, and waiting for the opening of the cradle-box through which they were to pass their respective children into the institution. It was a sad and degrading sight. The women looked apathetic and unmoved. One child, about two years of age, dressed in deep mourning, was leaning against a respectably dressed woman, and was sobbing most bitterly. We hoped the woman was not its mother, as she looked so calm and composed; and she did not even try to soothe the child, who appeared aware of its fate. They told us there were sometimes as many as sixty infants admitted in one day: many were sent in from the country towns and villages.

Three miles down the river, at the outside of the city of Lisbon, stands Belem Church. It was built by Don Manuel in 1500, in gratitude for the success of Vasca de Gamos's expedition. The interior of this church is a marvel of beauty, and of a peculiar style of architecture. You enter by a fine doorway at the west, and under low vaulted arches for two bays; it then opens out to its full height. The two centre pillars on each side are small and light, of pure white marble, elaborately carved; and these are of great height, and support the roof. One great peculiarity is, that the aisles, being of the same height as the nave, the arches of both these and the transepts are also of the same height, reaching to the very roof of the church. Two fine marble pulpits are placed at each side of the chancel; two more modern have been erected against the two side pillars, which are also elaborately and beautifully carved; the steps leading up to them are of different coloured marble. A modern chancel has been added in bad taste. The sacristia, which is about thirty feet square, has a vaulted roof, the centre of which is supported by a thin pillar rising out of a fountain. The tying of the roof in it and in the church is admirable. There is the appearance of a double-organ; but the pipes of it have been sold, and a cabinet-sized organ placed within for use. The Portuguese churches have not the large wooden choirs in the centre as in Spain, so that the whole is seen at one glance; and it has a much more noble appearance. We also, in Portugal, invariably found low altar-railings instead of the high and often handsome bronze or iron gates or *rejas*. They have a considerable space boarded over, and raised a few inches from the ground in front of the altar. Our guide told us it was for the ladies only to kneel upon, and no men are allowed to go there. There were eight doors of dark wood at the left side of the church, which are confessionals for the women. The men's confessionals are in a different part of the church. The cloisters are very rich, in the same ornate style. There are two tiers of arches; the lower are divided by three pillars, the centre one of which is twice as thick as the side ones. They are all richly and differently ornamented. The square of the cloister is peculiar; the four angles are all cut off and arched over. There are the remains of a small chapel, but the roof is quite gone.

MODERN AQUEDUCT.

The modern aqueduct in the highest part of the city is the grand work of a Portuguese nobleman one hundred and fifty years back. The water is conveyed from near Cintra through an aqueduct in which there are two ducts, in order that if one is out of order, the water may be shifted to the opposite, to admit of either side being repaired. It is arched over, and sufficiently high to permit a man to walk up between the two ducts and keep them in order. The tank is sixty feet deep, and the water is clear and green. This supplies the numerous fountains in Lisbon, at which you see hundreds of water-carriers and carts with oxen. It is still a great loss to the community that there are not pipes to convey the water into the houses, as from ten to fifty men are hourly employed at all the fountains carrying water to the neighbouring houses. These water-carriers are Gallicians, called here Gallegos.

Before closing our description of Lisbon, we are happy to state that the town once so notorious for the filth of its streets, is now beautifully clean, paved, and macadamised. The climate is mild, but variable, and the vicissitudes

PRIMITIVE VEHICLES.

are great. That part of the town called Buenos Ayres, where the English generally reside, has extensive gardens and agreeable residences; but it is far removed from the centre of the town, the markets, &c. There is a large and spacious English church, which is well attended, and generally full. Around it is a cemetery, with fine cypress and other trees in it, flowering shrubs, and many rare and beautiful plants. In this cemetery lie the mortal remains of Doddridge and several other distinguished men.

Some of the street carriages are antique and unique; they are lofty, and the shape of an old-fashioned sedan chair; they are fantastically gilded and painted. These carriages are perched upon the shaft, half-way between the wheels and the horse; they are, however, being fast superseded by comfortable, well-built, light carriages.

Fine oxen move about the streets with primitive-looking carts, the wheels of which are a solid block of wood without spokes, and the axles are fixed immovably in the wheels; the cart is then mounted upon this, and secured by two hoops, in such a manner that, as the cart moves forward, the axle and the two wheels all move round together with a creaking noise that can be heard half a mile distant.

Mules are a good deal used here, as in Spain; notwithstanding, we could seldom see a handsome pair in a carriage, and never without one or other having broken knees; whilst it is rare in Spain to see a horse with a broken knee.

One seldom sees a handsome man or woman in Portugal; the women's dress is, however, very respectable and neat: a dark cotton or silk dress, a black-cloth cloak, and a large square of thin white muslin, the size of a handkerchief, doubled, and pinned under their chins.

There are several new railways in course of formation throughout Portugal. It is a sufficiently rich country to be exceedingly improved by railway traffic; for some districts are as yet very unexplored, for there are very few roads, and even the mule-paths are rendered impassable in winter after rain. One of the railways in progress, and partly open, runs towards Badajos, at the south side of the river Tagus; another is open to Santarem, on the line to Coimbra and Leiria, on the north side of the river.

We went to Santarem, about thirty miles distant from Lisbon, by rail. We were two hours reaching it, and returned the same evening. Santarem stands on a high promontory, jutting out into the valley of the Tagus, by which the foot of the hill is washed. The view is magnificent and very extensive. It is a fine military position, and was held by Don Miguel as such for a long time. There are considerable Moorish remains here. The Alcazar (or castle) stands in a commanding situation, and several of the fine old churches have been built on the site of mosques. In the present century fourteen monasteries have been suppressed, and their fine churches left to fall into ruins, and in many instances desecrated and turned into magazines for wine and goods of every description. One particularly fine church is now used as a hay-loft for the cavalry horses; in it several of the tombs have been rifled, and the bones and dust of the dead cast on the ground around them ; a beautifully carved credence-table will soon share the same fate, as they are making a quarry of the grand old building, and selling the stones for a trifle. A Portuguese gentleman told us that the feeling was so strong against these monastic establishments, which had absorbed so much of the youth, energy, and the property of the country, that most of the inhabitants thought that those who assisted in pulling them to pieces were doing the State a service.

The Chapel of Santa Rita or Françesca is exceedingly interesting; in it is the tomb of Alonso, finely carved; also a part of a singular old monument, which for safety has been built into the wall ; and also a tomb of the Menezes; of the date 1147. There are four mosaics in blue and white porcelain, representing the Last Supper, the Israelites passing through the Desert, &c. &c. ; the date of these is 1779. They are very singular in their design, and in perfect preservation. Near the Plaza is the Jesuits' church and college ; at the latter two hundred students are at present receiving their education. In the chapel are some mosaics which are worth seeing, otherwise the building is not interesting. The hotel at Santarem is very indifferent, and the streets of the town are extremely dirty.

On our way going to and returning from Santarem, we had a fine view of the hills of Torres Vedras, where the Duke of Wellington constructed those fortifications which defied the French army. As we walked around Santarem, a Portuguese gentleman pointed out to us the olive-trees that spring in several stems from the root of those which the French army had cut down to light their fires.

The interior of Portugal is still a very unknown country to foreigners. We heard of magnificent churches and extensive Roman remains at such places as Thomar and Balalka, on the road to Leiria, which will now soon be accessible by railway.

We met an Englishman who had been twelve years in Spain and Portugal, and who is now directing the navvies on the railway which they are constructing between Santarem and Leiria, about sixty miles north-east of the former. He found the inhabitants wild and savage; but he had gained their confidence, and they would obey him, and do their work well. He paid them 1s. 8d. a-day, which was to them great wages. His workmen lived frugally; a sardine and a loaf of very indifferent bread served them for a dinner, and a cupful of soup, made merely of hot-water with bread crumbled into it, and flavoured with oil and garlic, for their supper. Yet notwithstanding this meagre fare, he was astonished at the amount of work they would accomplish in a day; and he found them steadier workmen than the Spaniards.

No one goes to Lisbon without visiting Cintra. This is a locality so charming in summer, as to make people regret that they have ties in other parts of the world. On leaving Lisbon there are some large villas and gardens in the suburbs; soon after, the bare heights of the hills are crowded with windmills; for some miles further, the country, although undulating, is bleak and uninteresting, with stone-fenced corn-fields, and this extends till you approach close to Cintra, which is fifteen miles distant from Lisbon. The corn-fields were green. The principal weed the farmers had to contend with appeared to be the pale bright-blue dwarf convolvulus, yellow and purple Irises, and a bright purple vetch, which grow in every direction. The rock of Lisbon and the hill of Cintra rise to a great height above the level of the sea. These hills attract the clouds and moisture of the Atlantic; and while at Lisbon all is arid and the air oppressive, there are at Cintra the most cool and refreshing breezes, and shade from the fine old forest-trees, and many streams and cascades; flowers and myrtles grow in the greatest profusion, and "the voice of the nightingale never is mute." In spring and winter Cintra is damp, but from this cause it is the more refreshing in summer. We were at an excellent hotel here, the Victoria. The landlady speaks English; her terms are very moderate, and everything is clean, and the food excellent. There are innumerable villas for great and small. All who can afford to leave Lisbon in the summer-time come out here. Some of the nobility have fine palaces and gardens.

The King of Portugal resides, during the summer months, in an old Moorish palace, which is more romantic than comfortable. It is kept in excellent order, and is at present undergoing some alterations. It is in Moorish architecture; the porcelain tiles in it are more raised and coarse than usually seen in Spain; many of them have a raised vine-leaf upon them. One large room is painted with magpies, another with deer, and a third with the arms of all the old Portuguese nobility. Families still bearing these arms are those who can boast of the best pedigree in Portugal. The mosaic floor of the chamber in which the lunatic King Alonso was confined by his wicked Queen is still very perfect; the tiles are worn where the unfortunate and restless monarch was chained.

The chapel, once a mosque, is very interesting; part of the roof is Moorish, the gallery opposite the altar is modern. In a large patio there is a fine Moorish bath in a recess, completely tiled round; when the water is laid on, it springs from innumerable jets in the wall, from the ceiling and from the floor, so as to converge and encircle the person standing in the centre of the recess. The kitchen is very peculiar; in it are two ranges for cooking with charcoal, above each of which there is a vast circular chimney, like one of our English glass-works, gradually narrowing at the top, and rising as high as a factory chimney. These completely overtop the whole palace, and we could only imagine that they were intended to carry off the fumes of cooking. These chimneys are about twenty feet in diameter at the bottom, and two feet at the top; these produced a most extraordinary echo of any noise made in the kitchen.

There are many rides and drives around Cintra; that to Colares, famous for its wine, is about four miles, and that **to** the Pena palace, the summer residence of the King's father, is about an hour's ride. The palace is on the summit of a high **hill** overlooking Cintra; the road to it is very steep, and winds up the hill-side, through pine, **brushwood**, and shrubs. You enter the palace by **a** gallery of arches which are cut out of the solid rock. The drawbridge is modern, **built** in 1840. Near this stands a very ancient cross **of the time of Don** Juan XIII. and his wife Donna Catalina. It was removed from the chapel on the summit of the hill by Don Manuel, who built the **present** palace, and who placed this cross **on** the huge boulder-stone at its entrance. The view from this palace is very extensive, overlooking the rock **of** Lisbon and the Atlantic to the west; the mouth of **the river Tagus, and** its yellow sandy beach, to the south; and to the east and **north,** the city of Lisbon, the hills of Torres Vedras, and the enormous palace of Mafra, which rises out **of** a flat green plain, and is about eighteen miles distant. The **Pena** palace is of Moorish architecture; it has of late **years been much restored, and** is still undergoing alterations. The rooms in it are numerous; one suite is comfortably furnished for present use. The chapel has an alabaster altar, above which, on a circular block of solid alabaster, which turns upon a pivot, are carved representations of the life of Christ. Although the road up to the Pena is so steep, the grounds around it are full of ravines and valleys, well wooded with forest-trees and shrubs, and ornamented with gardens and sheets of water.

There is a place called Monserrat, two miles from Cintra, the property of an English gentleman, which has great natural beauty, and is also laid out with great taste. There are extensive cork-woods around it; the garden is well watered; and there is a very valuable collection of tropical plants, ferns, and pines. The goa-pine is here a noble tree; its foliage is of a rich dark-green; and forms a striking contrast to the grey tint of the cork and olive trees around it.

On May the 7th, we embarked in a Peninsular and Oriental steamer for Southampton. In going down the river Tagus we passed the palace and church of Belem; a little beyond them a Moorish castle and a lighthouse, which have lately been put into excellent repair. The mouth of the river is commanded by fort St Julien, an old fortress. Soon after, we passed the rock of Lisbon and the heights of Cintra; the former rather projects out into the sea. Then we came in sight of Mafra, at the foot of the hills of Torres Vedras. A little further on, there is the singular isolated rock of Peneike, standing out of the sea like a castle; it was covered with innumerable sea-birds. The coast is low, and there is no object of great interest till you arrive near Oporto, which we unfortunately reached in the night, only remaining a few hours to take in passengers and merchandise, and leaving before sunrise. The next day, about one o'clock, we approached the picturesque and beautiful coast near Vigo, and soon after entered the bay, which is like a lake, being completely land-locked to the west by the rugged Bayona islands, which rise to a considerable height. It is a sheltered spot, and said to be a very fine climate.

The town of Vigo rises in terraces from the sea, and is surrounded by hills covered with verdure. This place would be a near and charming sanatorium for delicate people, if there was any accommodation for strangers, which there is not as yet; add to this that, in the most favoured parts of Spain, our countrymen meet with no favour or toleration from the miserable antiquated Government, or from the jealous and bigoted Church, which does not possess even the esteem or affection of its own people. An Englishman is neither allowed to worship his Creator while he lives, nor permitted a Christian burial in case of his death in their country. We knew an instance of a most estimable man who shared a very large fortune with the poor during his life, and when he died they said, " What a pity that so good a man could not go to heaven!" The Spaniards, like the Chinese, talk of their country as if their Government, and everything pertaining to it, was celestial, and we, and the rest of the world, as compared with them, barbarians! Do they not deserve to be taught the same lesson we taught the Chinese lately? We do not wish that they should suffer at our hands, or indeed at any other hands, but is Spain always safe from France or America? When she accumulates more wealth, will she be safer from France on the one hand, or is Cuba safe from America on the other? Spain is surely not in a position to despise our sympathy; but the

Spaniards, like the Chinese, do despise those who have not the power or the spirit to command respect. When will our Government demand that our church and creed shall be treated with the same respect and toleration in Spain that we accord to theirs in England? Before leaving Vigo, we shipped a very curious part of our cargo— namely, 400,000 fresh eggs for the English market. Early potatoes and other vegetables, pears, strawberries, and other fruit, are brought in large quantities from Lisbon and Vigo. We had strawberries daily at Lisbon in April, and green peas were very abundant.

We sailed out of the Bay of Vigo in the afternoon, and soon after prepared for the Bay of Biscay. We hoped that good fortune would attend us; but Æolus, who controls the winds with imperial sway, had resolved to give us a bit of a tiff. We had a strong head-wind for two days. It was a very disagreeable time. Some of the passengers suffered more than we did, but red eyes and yellow cheeks were marked features amongst us. Instead of being five days at sea, we were six and a-half. Those vessels that ply between Lisbon and Southampton are the slowest and smallest of the Peninsular and Oriental Company's boats. We met with much civility on board; the fare was abundant. We landed at eight o'clock on Sunday evening at Southampton, where we were very comfortable at Radley's Hotel. Next morning we proceeded to London, and were amused by having Waterloo stuck on each of our boxes. We hope that, out of politeness to our Gallic neighbours who may land here, the directors have a different label to put upon their effects. It was the first burst of summer, and after the wilds of Spain we were much struck with the beautiful garden-like cultivation and the fine forest-trees of the country. Soon after mid-day we arrived in London. No waste of time or life here. Assisted by energetic and active porters and policemen, in five minutes our luggage was all on the top of a couple of cabs. We were seated within, the doors were banged, and in a very short time, by the blessing of Almighty God, we were safe in the arms of those we loved dearly.

www.ingramcontent.com/pod-product-compliance
Lightning Source LLC
Chambersburg PA
CBHW020844160426
43192CB00007B/772